Finding The Story

Hard Texts,
Homiletical Narratives,
And Hearing God's Voice

James Ayers

CSS Publishing Company, Inc., Lima, Ohio

FINDING THE STORY

Copyright © 2007 by
CSS Publishing Company, Inc.
Lima, Ohio

The original purchaser may photocopy material in this publication for use as it was intended (worship material for worship use; educational material for classroom use; dramatic material for staging or production). No additional permission is required from the publisher for such copying by the original purchaser only. Inquiries should be addressed to: Permissions, CSS Publishing Company, Inc., 517 South Main Street, Lima, Ohio 45804.

The scripture quotations contained in this book do not come from any particular English Bible, but are exact quotes translated from the original Greek scriptures.

Library of Congress Cataloging-in-Publication Data

Ayers, James
    Finding the story : hard texts, homiletical narratives, and hearing God's voice / James Ayers.
      p. cm.
    ISBN-13: 978-0-7880-2445-0 (bound : alk. paper)
    ISBN-10: 0-7880-2445-0 (bound : alk. paper)
  1. Bible—Homiletical use. 2. Narrative preaching. I. Title.
    BS534.5.A94 2007
    251—dc22

2006102266

For more information about CSS Publishing Company resources, visit our website at www.csspub.com or email us at custserv@csspub.com or call (800) 241-4056.

Cover design by Barb Spencer
ISBN-13: 978-0-7880-2445-0
ISBN-10: 0-7880-2445-0

PRINTED IN U.S.A.

To Micaela

Table Of Contents

Introduction   7

Chapter 1   21
The Scriptures And The Power Of God
encountering the presence of God
when the preacher tells a story

Chapter 2   39
Narrative Freedom
following Jesus' pattern of creativity
when the preacher tells a story

Chapter 3   71
Love Songs And Love Stories
preaching psalms of praise as a story

Chapter 4   93
Hurl Their Babies Against The Rocks
preaching imprecatory psalms as a story

Chapter 5   117
To Make A Long Story Short
preaching multi-chapter texts as a story

Chapter 6   137
What Do These Words Mean?
preaching ancient Hebrew and
Greek root words as a story

Chapter 7   151
Once Before There Was A Time
preaching the doctrine of
predestination as a story

Chapter 8   177
If Only You Had Been Here
preaching the doctrine of death
and eternal life as a story

Chapter 9   193
I Am Sending You
preaching the doctrine of resurrection
and mission as a story

Chapter 10   211
Once Upon A Christmas
preaching the doctrine of incarnation as a story

Introduction

Once upon a time there was a teenage girl named Esther. She lived in the days when teens were expected to have the maturity and dependability that marriage requires. Esther, still about a month shy of her fourteenth birthday, was getting married this weekend to a boy named Bartholomew.

She was excited about it, and a little scared, too. This was an arranged marriage. In some arranged marriages the bride and groom never see each other until the wedding itself. But Bartholomew's family had fig and olive orchards. They sent shipments of olive oil and dried figs on the caravans to the big cities of Caesarea and Jerusalem. They came to Esther's village for the annual harvest bazaar. She had seen him there, and she had listened as her mother haggled with him over the price of olives. So she knew a little bit about him. She knew he was sixteen. She knew he was not the most handsome boy in the world, but he looked all right. She knew his family was not rich, but they were certainly not poor. And she knew she was marrying him this weekend.

Esther believed she would grow to love this young man Bartholomew, and she knew the wedding was going to be so lovely, with quite a feast afterward. She would learn how to be a wife and mother. She would be a good wife, she knew she would. She and Bartholomew would be happy. Part of her heart knew they would be happy, and part of her heart was so scared. She was thirteen, almost fourteen, and she was about to move out of her home and move in with this young farmer.

The wedding day came, a bright sky-blue day, and everyone in all the villages had come to wish her well. The flowers were perfect. The weather was perfect. And as for Esther herself — perhaps she did not look perfect, because who really can? — she knew she looked her best, and she knew every eye was on her as she walked, stately and demure, into the center of the gathering. Then she and Bartholomew said their promises, and at the end of the ceremony everyone raised a great shout of joy and the party began.

There was lots of food and lots of wine, and Esther felt dizzy, from the sun or from the wine, or maybe from the happiness she felt: maybe this was what being in love was about. Then she heard the murmuring. "They've run out of wine." You know how it is, when everyone's trying to smile and pretend that nothing's wrong, even though everybody knows that everybody knows? Esther was trying to keep on smiling, too. This was her wedding day, the happiest day of her life, and yet it was about to turn into this terrible humiliation. She saw the head caterer shaking his head, talking to his crew people. It was the caterer's job to *serve* all the food and drink, but it was up to Bartholomew and his family to *provide* all the food and drink. Now the wine had run out, and Bartholomew would be shamed. His whole family would be shamed. Everything would be ruined. This should be her day, her day of happiness, but she could feel Bartholomew's embarrassment, standing next to her. The only thing she could do was keep standing there, smiling and pretending everything was wonderful, even though she was dying inside.

She saw the servants doing something out in the courtyard, wrestling with the big water jars standing out there. Then one of them brought a wineglass to the head caterer. He burst forth in a big smile, called something across to Bartholomew, nodded to his crew people, and they began ladling wine out to everyone once again. Apparently they hadn't run out after all, they must have had some stored down in a cellar or something; it was going to be all right. She snagged a glass of wine off the tray of one of the waiters, and took a sip. Even though she was no wine expert, she thought it tasted pretty good. Esther's heart filled up with gladness at the goodness of life.

Once upon a time there was a fellow named Samuel. He was not afraid of hard work. He'd never been interested in business, and he'd never learned a trade. He might have ended up as a migrant laborer, hiring on to do whatever heavy manual jobs were needed, digging ditches or carrying loads, and then moving on to the next town when the work ran out in the last one. But he got himself hired by a family that ran a farm — a series of orchards, actually. They grew olives and figs. There was plenty of digging and carrying involved, but it was steady work, with a place to sleep each night and reliable meals.

The son in this family was getting married. Bartholomew was his name. The boy was just sixteen years old, but he had a good head on his shoulders, and it was already clear that when he inherited the business, he would run it well. That was something Samuel could tell by the way Bartholomew treated the hired help. Bartholomew expected Samuel to work hard, but he always gave him his instructions clearly, and he'd listen if Samuel had to explain why a job took longer than the original plan called for.

The wedding feast was in full swing, and they ran out of wine. Samuel could tell how awkward everybody felt, but he knew it wasn't his fault. Ordering the wine had never been one of his jobs. Then the mother of Jesus said to Samuel and several of the others, "Do whatever Jesus tells you." That was no problem for Samuel; he always did whatever anybody told him.

Jesus pointed to the six big clay water jars lined up at the edge of the courtyard. Each would hold twenty or thirty gallons. "Fill the jars with water," he said. Samuel knew the jars would weigh about 200 pounds each, once they were filled with water. He'd wrestled those jars, filled with water, many times before. He couldn't see how it would help, to carry those big old jars out to the well, and then fill them up, bucket by bucket, and then lug them back into the courtyard. What they needed was wine, not water. But Samuel wasn't afraid of hard work. All his life he'd done it, he'd done whatever job was called for. So Samuel said to a couple of the others, "Come on, let's get to it." They took the jars out to the well, filled them with water, and brought them back inside.

After they got the last jar in place, Jesus said to Samuel, "Now get a wineglass, and fill it, and take it to the head caterer." Samuel did it. He saw that it had turned purple, and that astonished him. His right hand shook a little as he ladled the wine, and some of the wine splashed onto his left hand, which was holding the wineglass. So as he carried the wine across the courtyard to bring it to the head caterer, Samuel switched the wineglass to his right hand, and surreptitiously licked the spill off his left hand. It was wine, all right, and even though he was no wine expert, he thought it tasted pretty good.

The head caterer *was* a wine expert, and when he tasted the wine Samuel brought him, he thought it tasted pretty good, too. He called across to Bartholomew, "You know, usually they serve the good wine first, and then they bring out the cheap stuff later. But wow! This is mighty fine wine you're providing for us." And Samuel wondered, "Am I supposed to tell him where the wine came from?"

Once upon a time there was a woman named Mary. She'd been a teenage bride herself once, many years ago, though now she was a wise and mature woman in her mid-forties. She had raised her family, five boys and three girls, and she was a grandmother many times over.

It's not so easy, taking care of such a big family, but she felt like she'd done pretty well, all things considered. She felt like she understood all her children except for one — the oldest, Jesus. All the rest of them were living their lives like normal people — except for Jesus. He'd always been different. Right from the time of the visions of angels, before he was ever born — and he was always so devout growing up. Well, Mary herself was devout. Many people were. Mary believed in God with real sincerity, she *believed*, but in all her life she had never encountered anyone who talked to God the way Jesus did. It was wonderful just to be there, when Jesus was praying.

Mary went to this wedding for these two teenagers, Bartholomew and Esther. They looked so young — so full of the eagerness of life — so full of promise. It was a day of great joy, until they ran out of wine at the reception.

Mary nudged Jesus. "Oh, no. Look! They've run out of wine."

You know how mothers don't always say everything with their words: sometimes they say it with their tone of voice? Sometimes your mother says something to you, and the tone of her voice means, "I'm not just giving you information here, I'm expecting you to do something about it." Do you know that tone, in your mother's voice? That was the tone in Mary's voice.

Jesus recognized that tone of voice.

You know how teenagers often react to the least little suggestion from their mothers with this strenuous exasperation? Then, when we grow to be adults, Mom can say something, and somehow we react with that same reaction, almost as if we are still teenagers. Apparently it was the same for Jesus. Because what he said was, "MO - THER - R - R - R! This just *isn't* the right time at *all*!"

And what did Mary do? Her response was to beckon to several of the servants, hook her thumb to point back at Jesus, and say, "Do whatever he tells you." Then Jesus did what his mother wanted.

This is a book about preaching. I suppose you have picked it up because you are interested in preaching — because you want to become a preacher, or perhaps because you want to become a better preacher.

Well, then, preacher, you may have noticed that from time to time people offer complaints about how sermons can be irrelevant and dull. You yourself have heard sermons that seemed pretty tedious; perhaps you have indeed lamented to yourself that your own preaching has felt kind of stale for the last little while.

So we might begin by noting that a person can tell a familiar Bible story like the wedding at Cana in John 2:1-11 from several different perspectives, and it is interesting the way it remains the same story and yet becomes quite different. Would that be a step in the right direction, then, if it turns out that offering contrasting perspectives on the same story might make a sermon more interesting?

That might indeed be a helpful improvement, but most preachers actually want to offer something more than "interesting." They want to believe — quite often they make the explicit claim — that God will be present in the sermons they preach. They say that during this time when the preacher is talking about the insights gathered from reading the Bible, God Almighty will speak to the souls of the gathered people in some definitive way.

Isn't this a strange notion? The Bible, this collection of stories and songs from times and places so foreign to today's life, how can it be that the words of this ancient text should touch people's hearts as the very word of God? Down through the centuries the Christian church has declared it over and over: that as people read this Bible, they would hear not only the words of human authors but also — especially — they would encounter the voice of God, discerned within their own souls.

Yet it is hardly self-evident, this claim that these ancient words should be the Word of God. Plainly enough, it cannot apply directly to the marks on the page or the sounds in the air. Plainly enough, there is nothing magical in the words themselves. How do we know this? We know this because all of us can give testimony of occasions when we have read or heard words from the Bible, and nothing happened.

One day we find the reading boring. Another day's excerpt may feel kind of intriguing, perhaps even captivating. Either way, it hardly qualifies as life-changing. Again, perhaps our mind wandered quite far afield while we were supposed to be listening. If somebody gave us a quiz tomorrow on today's Bible lesson, we would fail. Perhaps, instead, we would score well on such a quiz. We paid enough attention to repeat most of the details on demand. Yet once again, either way it would prove to be just another case of the material in a book that we remembered or didn't, as has happened with thousands of lessons we have encountered.

The bottom line remains the same in each of these instances: nothing particular happened. We would not claim that we encountered God in such moments, for we did not have any such experience of encounter. This is how it has happened for all of us, many times over.

What does this mean? It means that it is not possible to claim that any mere reading of the words of the Bible will necessarily do anything at all. The words themselves are not magic. Every single one of us can supply all the evidence necessary to prove this.

The belief lives on. In spite of this common indisputable experience, the belief lives on in the telling and retelling of the stories and songs from the Bible, people will genuinely encounter the presence of God.

Why is that?

It is because so many of us have indeed encountered the presence of God, in these very texts. We never know for sure how it will happen or indeed if it will happen. We are not in charge of this process. It helps to be attentive; yet sometimes when our yearning is the strongest, when our readiness is at its peak, we come up empty. Sometimes when we are dismissive and scoffing, the voice of God addresses us most clearly. There is nothing we can do to guarantee that it will happen, yet we discover, over and over again, that God does indeed speak to us, move our souls, and change our lives, through these ancient texts.

When Jesus presented his message to his followers, one of the things he did was to tell stories. As they have come down to us, a few of these stories are brief, and the rest are even briefer. When we read them, we find that even when telling a story that takes less than two minutes, Jesus could include some very unusual plot twists. On some occasions people heard the stories Jesus told and thought, "Hmm, that's interesting, but what's the point?"[1] Other times they got the point at once. They perceived that Jesus had told the story about them (Matthew 21:45).

It turns out that the story was about them all the time, even during the times when they did not recognize that. Jesus didn't tell stories just for entertainment value. He told stories so that people could hear the Word of God. This would happen as they listened to the story and discovered that it was a story about themselves and God.

We can listen to a story just for fun. We hear it a different way, though, when we recognize that it is a story about us. Perhaps we will come to recognize that part way through the story. Perhaps we hear the entire thing and never realize that we are in this story. Or possibly from the very beginning we will be deliberately attentive to this, even prayerful, asking, "Lord, where am I in this story? How is it that this ancient text is telling the story of my own life?"

What happens if I listen to the story of the wedding in Cana in the realization that this is a story about me? Perhaps I will hear the story of this girl who is getting married, and see how she is the recipient of grace even though she hasn't yet recognized this. Then I might ask myself, what if Jesus decides to work a miracle out at the edge of my awareness, and I don't even recognize it? Here comes Jesus, and he makes what could be a painful or embarrassing situation come out all right. What if Jesus is doing that, and I don't even notice? Perhaps the preacher will help me recognize this with an allusion to the story of the great patriarch Jacob, who had managed to live his life with little awareness of God, and then finally got it one morning as he woke up from his most vivid dream, and commented, "Surely the presence of the Lord is here: but I did not know it" (Genesis 28:16). Thus it could be that, in hearing the story of this young girl with a miracle taking place at her wedding, I will see that there are places in my life where I also might well identify signs of God at work. Yet, up until now I have not paid attention to where these blessings have come from.

There are many people like that in the world. Perhaps, as a preacher like you tells this Bible story, I will be one of them, sitting there in the sanctuary, and I will recognize that this is a story about me. Miracles of grace are happening, signs that the Lord is present, although I did not know it. Perhaps, then, in that moment, I will hear the voice of God whispering within my soul: "And yet you *could* know it — if you just recognized where that grace comes from."

But maybe not. Maybe I won't identify with that girl at all. It could be, instead, that I'll find my place in the story when I hear you talking about that solid hardworking servant, the kind who just goes ahead and does what needs to be done. People often don't pay much attention to the everyday workers who do the everyday work, but if I'm one of those everyday workers, I might identify with him right away. Maybe I'll feel a little frustrated by the way people always take us hard workers for granted. Within this very story, everyone is going to get impressed about the wonder of turning water into wine, but nothing's going to happen unless somebody brings the water. Perhaps my point of identification comes with the specific of the labor involved in hoisting big water jars that weigh a couple hundred pounds each. Maybe a lot of my work — within the life of the church or beyond it — feels just like that. Here's this faithful servant, working hard on his day off, and with the sweat running in his eyes it's hard to see just what all this heavy lifting is supposed to accomplish. It turns out there's a miracle on the schedule, a miracle that happens because of the grace of God, but this miracle also happens because of ordinary workers who go ahead and do this extra work that wasn't on their schedule at all.

There are many people like that in this world. Perhaps, as a preacher like you tells this Bible story, I will be one of them, sitting there in the sanctuary, and I will recognize that this is a story about me — one of the reliable workers. Miracles of grace happen because God is gracious and because of the hard work of people like me. That could be the moment when I hear the voice of God whispering within my soul, "Even when no one else seems to appreciate or even notice the extra effort you put in, I see it. Indeed, it is often your behind-the-scenes labor that I use, when I bring about the miracles that will bring blessings to people's hearts."

Again, maybe not. Maybe I won't connect with the story as the bride or the servant. Maybe I'll connect as you tell me the story of Mary.

There are just a couple of places in the Bible where someone says to Jesus, "What we need here, Jesus, is for you to work a miracle," and he answers, "I don't think so." Then the woman — both times it's a woman — doesn't give up when her petition doesn't get a positive answer. Instead, she finds a way to persevere, and she ends up seeing things happen the way she knew they should. The first is right here, when Mary tells Jesus about this need, and he answers: "It's not the right time." But she persists, and the miracle happens.

The second is the story of the Syrian woman whose daughter is ill (Matthew 15:21-28; Mark 7:24-30). When she shows up to ask Jesus to heal her daughter, he indicates that this is apparently not the right place for one of his miracles. His mission is to the children of Israel, and they are near Tyre and Sidon, well outside Galilee. He quotes a proverb, "You can't take the children's bread and feed it to the dogs." That may indeed have been a famous saying of the time. Yet, even if we can convince ourselves that it might not have sounded so harsh then as it does now, it still seems to be a pretty definitive way of saying, "No." But the woman doesn't give up. She comes back with a saying of her own, matching Jesus proverb for proverb: "Still, the dogs do get the crumbs that fall from the children's table." Jesus responds to her faithful persistence, and the miracle happens.

There are many people like that in this world. Perhaps, as a preacher like you tells this Bible story, I will be one of them, sitting there in the sanctuary, and I will recognize that this is a story about me. I have had experiences in prayer that have left me feeling dejected. I have asked for a miracle and Jesus apparently thought it was not the right time, or not the right place. And I have ended up walking away in futility. What will happen when you tell me the story of Mary, perhaps paralleled by a brief recounting of the story of the Syrian woman who asked Jesus to heal her daughter, and I listen as you wonder about how this prayer business works? Will I hear the voice of God, in the midst of this? There is no guarantee, but it could turn out that this becomes the moment when I hear God's invitation not to give up quite as quickly as I have in the past. If there have been two different occasions when a woman asked Jesus for a miracle and he said, "No," but she persisted, and in the end the miracle happened, then perhaps there are miracles that I will yet see, because I find the courage to persist in prayer even when the Lord starts out saying, "No."

This book is about narrative preaching. More specifically, it is about how a preacher can make use of narrative to illumine some of the harder-to-preach texts of the Bible.

You have already seen a hint of how this can work here in this introduction, as I have told the story of a portion of the Bible. The wedding at Cana is already a story, of course; all I have really done is presented a story that already comes to us as a narrative in its setting in the gospel. I have told it a little larger than the brief version John recorded for us; and as to the series of events that form the plot, I have noticed that these look a little different, from the differing perspectives of various individuals around Jesus in the story.

The thing to notice, for the moment, is that I have not *explained* the story of the wedding at Cana. I have not tried to give you background material about how first-century Galilean weddings took place, or what marriage meant within the culture of the day, so that you would *understand* the story better. I have simply recounted three brief versions of the same story — and invited you to listen and see what happens.

Sometimes what will happen, as you listen to the story, is that you will hear God speaking to you.

It is not always obvious how to use narrative when it comes to preaching from imprecatory psalms and psalms of praise or from texts that address important points of doctrine or from texts that depend on the root meaning of Greek and Hebrew words or from texts where Paul needed several chapters to form his argument. What I intend to show you is this: With tough biblical texts like these, you may well communicate more effectively if you can find and tell the story that lies behind that text.

Many other styles of preaching have been used quite effectively throughout the history of the Christian church. I have long been a fan of the two-hour doctrinal sermons of the English Puritans, with their detailed demonstrations of how God's astonishing grace is revealed in scripture and applied in our lives. This was, apparently, quite successful. People found their hearts greatly moved, people learned the content of their faith in considerable depth, people were comforted and sustained by the presence of God. Certainly there is a level of comprehension that is available when the preacher has the scope to present a great deal of material, carefully outlined and referenced. The hearer gains immensely from this. Perhaps the time will come again when such detailed doctrinal preaching is again the norm. Indeed, when people are dissatisfied with a preacher who offers explanations that only take a single hour, because our hearts long for those two-hour discourses.

Verse-by-verse exposition has an equally impressive pedigree, stretching from Augustine and Chrysostom through John Calvin and into modern times; indeed, this was the style of preaching they taught me during my own seminary days. Yet, I confess that I have not personally experienced much success in creating the same strength in a twenty-minute exegesis of scripture that I see when I read the discourses of the masters. It may simply be that what a preacher can do effectively in an hour or two cannot be done in twenty minutes. It may be that times and cultures have changed to such an extent that people no longer have the ability to follow a closely reasoned oral presentation for two hours, and indeed no longer have the ability to follow such a presentation for twenty minutes.[2]

It is sometimes noticeable, in the work of the expository and doctrinal masters, that they have taken a text of scripture that is a story from first to last and have turned it into a lesson in exegesis. This is not just a fault of those from days gone by. Preachers today just as often take quite an interesting story out of the biblical text and turn it into a rather pedestrian recital of explanations and exhortations.

And yet in its essence, a sermon is not about explanations as and exhortations, but about hearing the word of God and responding in faithfulness. This is true when the biblical text in question is itself a story, and it remains true when Sunday's text is drawn from an epistle or an imprecatory psalm. This book proceeds on the hope that as the preacher tells the story, the members of the congregation will hear the word of God addressing them, and will find their own hearts responding with devotion to God.

Each chapter includes three kinds of material:

1. Each chapter includes a few brief exercises, to help you work through the notions that have been presented. Some of these will require only a few minutes to make something experientially clear, while others will take more time but will reward the preacher who does them with the solid beginnings to a number of sermons.
2. Each chapter includes a certain amount of explanation, woven into the rest of the material. A sentence or two of background or analysis, a few words to contrast one idea against another one. This sort of thing often proves to be quite helpful for people.
3. Each chapter includes quite a bit of narrative. As to how that works: well, after you finish the exercise here, turn to chapter 1, and you'll see.

Exercise

Consider other possibilities for telling the story of the wedding at Cana. Imagine, for example, what the story would be like if it were told from the perspective of:

- the groom;
- the bride's mother;
- the caterer; or
- the water that gets turned into wine.

Choose one of these, and take a couple of minutes to tell the story of the wedding at Cana from this perspective. You might feel that in order to do that you would need to study the passage for a while and take notes and work it out in detail, but, no. Don't do any of that right now. Instead, just pick one of those characters, and begin. Don't pause. Just start telling the story. Now.

---

1. The parable of the four soils (Matthew 13:3-8; Mark 4:3-8; Luke 8:5-8) tells the story of a farmer sowing grain in different spots around the field, and what resulted from that. The disciples recognized that they didn't get it, and so they asked further questions (somewhat in Matthew 13:10, more obviously in Mark 4:10 and Luke 8:9). The explanation of this parable (Matthew 13:19-23; Mark 4:14-20; Luke 8:11-15) tells us that the story isn't just about different kinds of soil, it's about people as they respond in various ways. In the midst of this we get an invitation (Matthew 13:9; Mark 4:9; Luke 8:9) "if you have ears, then hear" — which indicates to us that getting the point of what Jesus was up to depends on "hearing" it a particular way.

2. Neil Postman's fine essay *Amusing Ourselves to Death* (Penguin, 1985) examines the capability of the 1850s general public to appreciate and grasp the lengthy oral argumentation of the Lincoln-Douglas debates, and laments that this capability has been killed off as television has taught our culture to be moved, impressed, or entertained by brief series of images.

Chapter 1

The Scriptures And The Power Of God

encountering the presence of God when the preacher tells a story

  Caleb looked at his friends. They seemed to be having a pretty good time as they engaged in animated conversation with one another. All he could feel was the weight in his chest. He saw the laughter in their eyes, the sense of keen anticipation. He wanted to feel that same eagerness, but this dull ache in his soul kept getting in the way.
  Caleb had always expected life would feel better than this. He had grown up in a privileged family. He had the benefits of a good education. He was making decent money in the market. Many of his friends complained about tensions in their home life, but Caleb and his wife still got along pretty well. Their children were doing fine in school, yet something was missing. He didn't know what it was.
  Sometimes he thought it might be religion. Part of his soul genuinely wanted to be religious. Yet Caleb couldn't quite bring himself to believe all those Bible stories about how God works in people's lives in powerful and miraculous ways.
  No one in his circle of friends believed those Bible stories. It was a tight circle of friends. In those days your circle of friends and your political party and your religious denomination and your social set were all the same. It made for lots of close contact. People knew what was going on in one another's lives. That could be good. It meant people were there to care for each other, in time of need. But it also meant nobody rocked the boat by questioning "the way we've always done it."

Caleb's group was known as the Sadducees. It was a political party and a distinct segment of society, but it was also a religious group — even though they didn't do a lot of the things that religious people commonly do. The Sadducees didn't do things like devoting time every day to studying scripture or following a discipline to strengthen their life of prayer or striving to do acts of mercy with cheerfulness, but they still wanted to be religious. They still wanted to feel the sense of purpose and wonder that religion is supposed to provide.

Caleb had thought about this situation quite a bit. As he had thought about it, he believed that he had come up with the reason it felt so awkward. What it came down to, as Caleb saw it, was this: He and his friends wanted religious meaning without religious content. He and his fellow Sadducees had mostly dismissed the sacred text that had provided the substance for their people's faith down the centuries. That created this challenge: Where could they turn to discover the meaning of their lives, after they had discarded the source of meaning? Can you have religious meaning without religious content? Maybe you could, but Caleb suspected the answer would turn out to be "No, you can't have religious meaning without religious content." And where would that leave Caleb and his friends who had rejected the content of a faith that speaks of how God touches human lives?

Sometimes it seemed to Caleb that all the Sadducees had left was entertainment. From our present-day perspective we can see that this was not unique to them. All down the centuries people have looked to entertainment to find life's meaning. Here in America we have built a vast entertainment industry, to sell the idea that the joy of life happens while you sit and watch. We sit and watch sports, movies, and television, and seek life's meaning in these entertainments that the industry has provided.

In earlier times, though, people had to make their own entertainment. Caleb watched his friends as they planned out how to do that. The current scheme had to do with how to have some fun at the expense of some preacher from the north country who had come to town. They had made fun of his name — Jesus or Freezes or Sneezes, something like that. They had made up songs about him:

> *Jesus puts his money in the Bank of Galilee.*
> *Jesus puts his money in the Bank of Galilee.*
> *Jesus puts his money in the Bank of Galilee.*
> *Jesus saves! Jesus saves! Jesus saves!*

Yet, while they were feeling superior, this hayseed Galilean preacher had gathered quite a following. So Caleb's friends, Dan and Joel, had come up with the idea of going to one of the meetings, and pretending to be really interested in his message. Then they would pose him a problem in biblical interpretation, and he'd get all embarrassed when he failed to resolve it.

The book of Deuteronomy gave the ancient Israelites an instruction that sounds strange to our present-day ears. It told them that when a man died childless, his brother had to marry the widow and raise up children for his deceased brother, so that the dead man's name wouldn't die out from the earth. Caleb listened as his friends constructed a case study. "Let's see," they plotted. "We'll say there were these two brothers" — "How about three brothers?" — "No, let's make it seven brothers," said Joel. "That's good, yes, seven brothers," everyone agreed. So with these seven brothers, the oldest brother marries this woman, but he dies before he has children. Then brother number two marries her, and he dies without children. Brothers number three, four, five, six, seven, all the same.

They decided to set up the tale as a great, long, shaggy dog story, using the same patterned phrasing as they went through each stanza of the story. As they recounted each brother's wedding to this woman, they would have the rabbi nod sagely once again as he quoted the passage from Deuteronomy 25. They would tell about the house of each successive brother, with a garden in the back where the family's cherished prize-winning onions were grown. They would tell about how the village women cooked the tastiest soup for the wedding feast, made each time from onions that had been grown in the backyard of this particular bridegroom's house. Finally, after seven long stanzas, telling one-by-one the story of each brother, they would arrive at the crux of the narrative where the woman herself finally died. Then they would pose their triumphant question: "Now, when they all get to heaven, Jesus, whose wife will she be?"

Caleb and his fellow Sadducees already knew the answer. Nobody gets to heaven — you die, you're buried, that's the end. But because this country preacher from Galilee believed in heaven, he'd have to declare whose wife she would be. He'd have to pick somebody, the oldest brother, or maybe the youngest one. And then they'd scoff, "But that's so arbitrary. What about the other six brothers?" And the preacher would be baffled and speechless, and they'd all laugh at him.

About eight or ten of them headed on downtown to the meeting. They were so ready to laugh. This was going to be so good. They knew they had to hide their smirks. In order to make this work, they couldn't give it away too quickly. They had to keep their sarcasm masked behind the pretense that they truly wanted to understand.

Now, in other places in the gospel, it tells how some of the most religious people got so upset with Jesus that they set themselves as his enemies. In their rage, they accused him of being the friend of outcasts and sinners (Matthew 11:19; Luke 7:34). They were mad that Jesus didn't maintain the proper superior attitude over the dregs of society. It almost gives us the feeling that these people might have been able to approve, if Jesus simply wanted to do good for the poor wretches at the bottom of the social ladder. But he went ahead and *liked* those people. With laughter and congeniality he visited them and ate meals with them, apparently because he enjoyed their company. His enemies knew there had to be something wrong with a person who willingly associated with those worthless folks at the margins of the community. Jesus! Phaugh! He's the friend of outcasts and sinners! That's what they said about him.

Caleb recognized this accusation as a deliberate and nasty slur, yet it didn't seem to bother Jesus. He went on liking those outcasts. He went on being the friend of sinners.

That was puzzling. But there was something even more puzzling. How do you respond to those who make deliberate nasty slurs in your direction? The baffling thing Caleb had heard was this: Even when people were out to get him, Jesus still seemed to care about them. His attitude toward his accusers seemed not to be condemnation but compassion. It was as if Jesus had decided to be not only the friend of sinners, but the friend of his enemies as well.

Caleb didn't understand that part. Most of those Galilean peasants didn't have much formal education, but they often made up for that with a certain native shrewdness. Caleb expected Jesus would have his fair share of this shrewdness. Caleb expected Jesus would have the prudence to see that it's not smart to be a friend to your enemies. Although Caleb hadn't told the others, he expected Jesus would have the insight to recognize that their group of Sadducees was out to embarrass him. He'd be shrewd — perceptive enough to discern the mockery hidden behind their false interest. Maybe he'd match them, sarcasm for sarcasm. Or maybe he'd simply ignore them.

The group of them made their way to the front of the crowd. They stood there together, and Joel spoke up and said, "Excuse us, Mr. Preacher, but we've got a real problem here, and we wonder if you could help us." He told the story they'd made up of the seven brothers, with all the details and trimmings. It took almost ten minutes to recite the whole thing. Caleb felt the restlessness stirring in the crowd. Some people muttered, "Get to the point." Others recognized what was happening and whispered to each other, "It's a trap, they have set this up to ridicule Jesus."

Jesus himself apparently didn't see it coming. He simply stood there, nodding with polite attention, as Joel recounted stanza after stanza of the tale they had made up about these seven brothers who had all married this woman.

Caleb thought, "Jesus doesn't get it. We're out to make fun of him. I had guessed he'd have the shrewdness to pick up on that. Oh well. Kind of disappointing."

Then Joel posed the stumper. "So, Jesus, help us understand this. Whose wife will she be?"

There was a pause. Standing there next to Caleb, Dan snickered. Then he nudged Caleb with his elbow and murmured, "We've got him now." Jesus looked at the group of Sadducees. He seemed to look right into the soul of each one of them. Jesus looked at Joel, at Dan, and at each of the rest of them. He looked at Caleb. As their eyes met, Caleb saw it. He saw that Jesus had seen from the beginning how they intended to trap him, how they wanted to entertain themselves by making fun of him. But for some reason Jesus hadn't gotten intimidated or resentful about that. Why not? As he asked himself that question, Caleb saw the answer. Jesus was the friend of sinners and the friend of his enemies, and he would be the friend of Sadducees, too. He liked those sinners, he liked those enemies, and he liked those Sadducees, even though he knew from the start that their plan was to humiliate him.

Jesus looked at them, as a friend who genuinely cared about them, and he asked, "Isn't this why you get it wrong — because you don't know the scriptures, and you don't know the power of God?"

Caleb was astonished at the gentleness in Jesus' voice as he said it. He could hear in his mind's ear just how harshly Jesus could have said those very same words, just how much scorn Jesus could have used in rebuking him and his friends. Surely that's what they deserved. But Jesus, the friend of Sadducees, had managed to speak with quiet compassion when he responded, "Isn't this where the problem comes from — it's because you don't know the scriptures, and you don't know the power of God?"

Caleb wondered, "How did he know the yearning of my heart? He understands that we Sadducees have trapped ourselves, with our desire for religious meaning without religious content."

Jesus, the friend of Sadducees, said, "Isn't this why you keep getting it wrong — because you don't know the scriptures, and you don't know the power of God?" And then he paused. He paused and left that question hanging in the air. "Isn't this why you are wrong — because you don't know the scriptures, and you don't know the power of God?"

And during the silence of that pause, in his soul Caleb heard God's voice whispering, "And yet, you could. You could know the scriptures. You could know the power of God."

When most preachers read this passage (Mark 12:18-27, paralleled in Matthew 22:23-32), they reckon that Jesus must have been quite angry with the Sadducees. They sense that in response to their scheme to humiliate him, Jesus scolded them for their lack of religion. It is certainly possible to read this passage this way. It is not the only possibility, however.

It would certainly help to hear Jesus' tone of voice as he spoke to the Sadducees here. The text, as it comes to us, contains no aural cues, no notations about how Jesus spoke. Were his words loud or soft, fast or slow? We do not know. One thing we must particularly recognize is this: There are no indications about the emotive coloring in his words. When people are bitter, when they are enraged, when they are discouraged, when they are excited, these emotions show up in their voice tones and in their gestures and body language as well. But for now we will restrict ourselves to the emotional coloring present in the actual sounds of the words. When we are in a conversation, we listen to the voice tones of the other people to understand what they mean, and we convey our own intentions the same way.

Exercise 1-1

Imagine that you are a young teenager who has just been told that the family is going on a trip to Grandmother's house next weekend. You get to use nothing but the two-word phrase "all right" to express your response.

1. Assume that you have been hoping to go to Grandmother's for several weeks, but circumstances have prevented it from happening and your response is the culmination of long waiting. Express your response out loud using only the two words "all right" conveying to your parents how glad you feel that this trip is happening at last.
2. Assume that you have plans of your own for next weekend, and this messes them up completely. You would like to argue against this trip. However, the arrangements for the visit to Grandmother's have been established and you

have no choice. You are frustrated and angry, but you know you must acquiesce. Express your response out loud. Convey to your parents how upset this trip makes you, using only the two words "all right."
3. Assume that going to Grandmother's is the most boring thing you can think of. You have no particular plans, but almost anything would be more interesting than this. Express your response out loud using only the two words "all right" to convey to your parents how dreary this trip sounds to you.

Some of you just skimmed through that exercise in silence, without saying the words out loud, thinking you didn't *really* have to do it out loud. Tsk, tsk. Go back now and do the exercise for real. When you read words off the page in silence, that's a different kind of event than when you say words out loud. As a preacher, you know that this is true. Preaching is, after all, an aural means of communication. It happens when you say words out loud, and people listen to the sounds you make. No matter how good your sermon may be, *preaching* will not happen if you stand there on Sunday morning in the pulpit and silently read your manuscript to yourself. If you are hoping that people will listen to the things you say, you need to listen first, and you need to know how the things you say are affected by the voice tones you use.

I really am serious about this. Go back and do the three parts of this last exercise. It won't take all that long. Actually, it's kind of fun. Say the words "all right" out loud each time, and deliberately listen to the difference it makes when you speak with the voice tones that indicate the emotions of excitement, anger, or boredom.

The story of "Jesus and the Sadducees who Told the Tale of the Seven Brothers" comes to us in just ten verses. It takes less than a minute of silent reading to get through it. Yet, the event itself was a conversation. It surely ran significantly longer than that, and it took place with people talking out loud. Those who were present could hear the tones in the voices, but those voice tones are not recorded for us. A major part of the meaning of this story is carried in the emotional coloring of the way the words were spoken out loud, and this is information that is only available when we listen to the words as spoken out loud. This information is not carried by the words as printed on the page.

Exercise 1-2

In Mark 12:24, Jesus begins to respond to the Sadducees' story. A fairly literal rendering of the verse would be:

> *Jesus said to them, "Isn't this the reason you go astray: because you know neither the Scriptures nor the power of God?"* — Mark 12:24

1. Assume that Jesus felt angry at the Sadducees for trying to trap him, and scornful of their ignorance of the Bible and their lack of religious experience. Read Mark 12:24 out loud, putting all the contempt you can into your voice tones.
2. Assume that Jesus felt compassion for these Sadducees, and was wistful because they had trapped themselves in their desire for religious meaning without religious content. Read Mark 12:24 out loud, putting all the affection you can into your voice tones.

At the risk of restating the obvious, the words you read aloud were exactly the same in both parts of the exercise, yet the meaning was considerably different. What made the difference? It is the tone in Jesus' voice, as he said the words.

How does the preacher know which way to say these words, then? How you will read this to the congregation, and how you will preach your sermon, depend on this question. There are three parts to the answer.

1. The first is to be deliberate in noting that as we read a text like this, we make interpretive decisions. If we reckon that Jesus felt bitter toward the Sadducees, or if we reckon that Jesus felt

compassionate toward the Sadducees, we are assessing or discerning or deciding which way of reading the passage makes the most sense or seems right to us.

Notice this. It is not the case that one way is simply a "straight" reading of the story, while the other is an "imaginative" or "alternative" paraphrase. Both of these possibilities are "straight" readings which take Jesus and the words he spoke quite seriously. As we work through this story, we draw on what we know from the rest of the gospel, and we make an inference about how Jesus felt about the Sadducees. Then we understand the story on that basis. We may be paying attention to the fact that there is more than one way of reading the story, and purposefully choosing the one that we think fits the best. Or we may simply take the first one that occurred to us without considering whether other options might work better.

In ordinary conversation, people routinely say things that turn out to be ambiguous. Husbands and wives are especially famous for this, but it also happens pretty often in business meetings, at family reunions, and in church committees. You say something, meaning one thing by it, and I take it to mean something else. Perhaps I take it to be a rather irritating comment on your part. (I may have been irritated already by something else — my personal context — or by my recollection of some of the irritating things you have said in the past — our shared context.) I react to this irritation, and you become offended that I am responding badly to your innocuous comment. As we all know, this sometimes turns into the kind of argument from which relationships never recover. Then again, we might recognize that we could be misinterpreting each other's remarks. If we do, then we have various question-and-answer possibilities for sorting through the confusion. When you said thus and such, did you mean...? Oh, you didn't? You meant something quite different, namely...? Ah, I see. Sorry. I misunderstood you, and responded badly as a result.

Ambiguities like that happen all the time in conversations with friends and relatives with whom we share a common history, culture, experience, and language. We should expect to encounter similar ambiguities when we read texts written thousands of years ago. We may notice these ambiguities and thoughtfully select the interpretation that makes the most sense to us, or we may simply stumble inadvertently into one option or another. But we will end up, again and again, on one side or another of an interpretive choice. That's neither good nor bad. It's just a fact. Still, it's usually better to choose thoughtfully rather than inadvertently.

2. The second issue is one of exegesis. When we are reading this story in an English Bible — which is the way almost all of us do our Bible reading, almost all the time — we are looking at a text that has translated for us the Greek words of the gospels, which are themselves a rendering of a conversation that most likely took place in Aramaic. We must reckon, then, with the fact that the words of this story have been interpreted from Aramaic to Greek, and then from Greek to English. As Christian preachers, if we want to know both the scriptures and the power of God, we will do our best to understand the original meaning of the text.

In this instance, we can see that the translators of English versions of the Bible have had to make interpretive decisions as they proceeded, just like everyone else. In Mark's telling of this story, he rounds off his account with a brief phrase (πολυ πλανασθε, Mark 12:27) that the English translators have rendered for us in words that could sound fairly stern — "you are quite wrong" (RSV, NRSV) — or even rather harsh — "you are badly mistaken!" (NIV).

Yet in the passive construction that we find here, πλαναω gives us a general meaning of "to go astray" or "to be mistaken or misled." Simply as a question of translation, it could equally well be rendered as something like "you have gone so far astray" or "you have let yourselves be seriously misled."

What that tells us, then, is that we should not jump to the conclusion that Jesus had an angry rebuke of the Sadducees in mind. That may well be exactly what Jesus intended. If we could hear his voice tones, we would know for sure. But within the Greek word πλαναω itself, there is nothing that tells us explicitly whether Jesus conveyed compassion or condemnation to the Sadducees here.

Exercise 1-3

Test the difference that voice tones make in rendering the meaning of πολυ πλανεσθε into English.

1. Assume that Jesus felt quite upset toward the Sadducees and intended to rebuke them strongly. Say (out loud) the words of this phrase, putting scorn and anger into your voice, as you use the NIV's wording:

    You are badly mistaken! — Mark 12:27

2. Assume that Jesus felt quite compassionate toward the Sadducees and yearned for them to encounter God's grace. Say (out loud) the words of this phrase, putting longing and wistfulness into your voice, as you use this alternative wording:

    You have let yourselves be seriously misled.
    — Mark 12:27

3. Now test the way your voice tones change the meaning when the phrase itself does not change. Say (out loud) the following translation first in scorn and then in wistfulness. Alternate back and forth several times between the two ways of saying this phrase, just to help yourself hear the contrast.

    You are so wrong. — Mark 12:27

There are times when careful exegesis in the original languages of scripture will enable us to say, with substantial probability, that an ambiguity in the text should be resolved in one direction and not in another. That will sometimes confirm and sometimes correct the impression we have picked up from our favorite English translations. When it happens that way, we become much clearer on the point of a given passage.

At other times, such as this one, study of the Greek text serves to demonstrate that a technical analysis of the words themselves will not resolve the ambiguity. As we endeavor to draw the meaning out of the words of the passage, we discover helpful insights. We find out as well that the vocabulary of the text does not establish that the meaning must be this and cannot be that. It may feel frustrating to do language study and then not come up with a unique answer, but it is also a worthy gain to recognize clearly that the words themselves within a passage carry an ambiguity.

3. As we seek to understand which way to understand a given passage of scripture, the third thing that must be said is this: The preacher has to listen to Jesus.

To recap: as preachers we need to recognize, first, that we are routinely going to make interpretive decisions, as we read the text of scripture. We want to do that, second, on the basis of the best exegesis we can muster. Third, as we do these two things, we must pay attention to hear what Jesus says to us.

I suppose that all of us have heard preachers make ringing declarations about things that "God told me" that have later proven to be so wrong. I certainly don't want to be counted among them, so arrogant in their supposition that they have heard better than anybody else. Yet, awkward as it feels, the doctrine of the word of God instructs us that our Lord will indeed speak to us through these words recorded in scripture.

If that doctrine is mistaken, is there any point in being a preacher?

If, instead, that doctrine is correct, if in the midst of scripture we will indeed experience the word of God speaking to our own souls, then we need to get over the embarrassment and listen for that voice, for ourselves, text by text.

Thus it falls to you, preacher, to ask in all deliberateness, "Jesus, what is it that you would say to me, through this passage? Sometimes I get lost in one of those Sadducee moments, where I still feel the longing for some religious meaning but don't seem to be connecting with the religious content. If I were one of the Sadducees in the crowd there, if you raised that question to help me listen to it, if you wondered with me whether the reason I don't get it is that

I don't know the scriptures and I don't know the power of God, how would I hear you saying it?"

Then listen.

If you're not quite sure what you're hearing, read the passage out loud again, and listen again. Here's an exercise to help you do that.

Exercise 1-4

Read Mark 12:18-27 out loud several times, from the English Bible you usually use.

1. Pretend you are an old grandmother, frail in health, sharing this story with your young grandchildren. Read through the text out loud, twice, first on the assumption that Jesus was angry, and then again on the assumption that Jesus was neither caught off guard nor enraged, but saw this as an opportunity to invite even those Sadducees to discover the scriptures and the power of God. Pay attention to the timbre of your voice, to how you speed up and slow down, to the places where you are loud or soft or silent. The point is to convey, with the sound of your voice, that you are this grandmother, and that you are telling the story of Jesus.
2. Pretend you are a teenager, a member of a scout troop, on a camping trip, where you have been appointed chaplain for this evening's campfire. You are nervous about this task, but you believe that this story can speak to the hearts of your fellow scouts. Read through the text out loud, twice, first assuming that Jesus was angry, then assuming that Jesus was inviting the Sadducees to discover the scriptures and the power of God. Again, pay attention to what you sound like, and to how different voice tones help you or get in the way as you tell this story.
3. Pretend you are a well-known local orator, strong of voice, one who doesn't need any microphones, confident of your abilities, and maybe a little pompous. You are to tell this story for the church's Labor Day picnic program. Do it

twice, as before: first assuming that Jesus was scolding the Sadducees for their lack of knowledge, and then a second time, on the assumption that he hoped they would decide to act on the basis of their longing to know the scriptures and the power of God.

By now you've listened to the sound of this passage quite a few times. You've heard Jesus speaking, alternating between a confrontational and an invitational tone of voice. Where in this process did you most clearly hear Jesus speaking to you?

As you answer that question, two follow-up questions emerge. The first is this: What will you do in response to that? That's the most important of the two questions, in terms of your own religious life. I can give you no advice about that; it's between you and Jesus to work out what your response needs to look like.

The second follow-up question is this: How will you tell the story of Jesus and the Sadducees, so that the congregation also can hear the voice of Jesus speaking to them? That's the most important of the two questions, in terms of your work as a preacher. Here I do have some advice, and since I expect you to be bold enough to offer your best to your congregation, let me be bold enough to offer you my best insight here.

God has given us these two gifts, the scriptures and the power of God, a gift of word and a gift of deed, so that we can hear what God says and experience what God does. These two gifts could change the lives of people like the Sadducees of long ago and people like the members of your congregation. They could change the lives of any of us, when we get ourselves trapped in the quest for religious meaning without religious content, for any of us who find ourselves desperate for entertainment to provide the joy of life while we sit and watch. Jesus asks us, "Isn't this where the problem comes from — because you don't know the scriptures, and you don't know the power of God?" And then he pauses, so that we can hear the quiet whisper in our souls, "But you could. You could hear God speaking to you through the scriptures. You could experience God's powerful activity in your own life."

As a preacher, you want your congregation to know that these two gifts, the scriptures and the power of God, have been given to us. You want to do your best to give them the opportunity to hear that, even while you recognize that you do not control the process. You want to do your best to be a servant, providing an occasion for members of the congregation to encounter God. Yet you do this, in the knowledge that the word God addresses to someone's soul is spoken by God, not by you. The power that God expresses in someone's life is expressed by God, not by you.

In the end, it's not about the text, it's not about the preacher, it's not about preaching style. All of these things are pointers, but they do not point to themselves, they point toward an encounter with God. They invite people to recognize Christ's voice addressing them in their own experience.

To sum up:

1. As a preacher, you want you and your congregation to know the scriptures and the power of God.
2. As a preacher listening to the words in scripture, you need to recognize that you will constantly be making interpretive decisions about what the text says and means.
3. As a preacher listening to the words in scripture, you need to pay attention to insights available to you from exegesis of the original languages.
4. As a preacher listening to the words in scripture, you need to actually *listen*, because some of the meaning of the text is carried in the emotional coloring of the words.
5. As a preacher, you want to hear the story of Jesus within this Sunday's text, with a lively attentiveness that prompts you to be ready to hear his voice speaking to you.
6. As a preacher, you want to tell the story of Jesus within this Sunday's text, with a lively attentiveness that prompts the congregation to be ready to hear his voice speaking to them.

I hope these six points are clear. Along with the narrative came a fair amount of explanation and analysis to try to make them clear.

But did you notice, most of what I have done in this chapter is to tell you the story of "Jesus and the Sadducees who Told the Tale of Seven Brothers" as a story experienced from the perspective of one of those Sadducees. And even though I did not follow the six-point outline, you got the material just fine. Along the way, you may indeed have felt the prompting of the Spirit encouraging you to know the scriptures and the power of God.

Still, I have done something here that may have made you a little uncomfortable. I have spun out this story in far more detail than either Matthew or Mark provided in their versions. I have provided a name for one of Sadducees, listed some of his friends, and included a set of anxieties and some reflective psychologizing. I even sang a song (to the tune of "The Battle Hymn Of The Republic," if you'd like to sing it to your congregation some day). You may have found that song a little irreverent, although, as an example of the disparagement the Sadducees were feeling, it's surely quite mild.

Perhaps you are wondering whether exercising that much narrative freedom is really legitimate. That's a fair question. Let me say a few things about that in chapter 2.

Chapter 2

Narrative Freedom

following Jesus' pattern of creativity when the preacher tells a story

Once upon a time there was a girl named Naomi. She grew up knowing that life can be very hard. But it wasn't until she turned fifteen that she found out how very hard it could be.

There were just four of them at home by then. Naomi's father had died four years earlier, a couple of months before her baby sister was born. Her older brother had gotten married a year before that, and her older sister the following spring. Good matches for both of them. They had moved away to start families of their own. Now it was just Naomi, her mother, and her two younger sisters in the little house. They existed by gleaning and scavenging. Sometimes two or three days would go by with nothing to eat, until they happened to get something. Hunger was their constant companion.

On the morning of Naomi's fifteenth birthday, her mother sat her down for a serious talk. She explained what Naomi already knew: there was no money, no dowry, no marriage in her future. They could not repay what they had borrowed from the moneylenders. From time to time they had received some small help sent by Naomi's older brother and sister, even though their own small families were barely scraping by. It was impossible to expect more from them. They faced starvation. They had no income. They had no expectations. They had no hope.

There was just one possibility. A slave owner who ran a brothel in the capital was willing to buy Naomi. He had offered sixty pieces of gold. It was an enormous amount of money. Eighteen pieces would pay off the family's debts. With careful management, four pieces a year would supplement what her mother and two sisters could make by gleaning, and keep them alive. In the end, then, that might leave about twelve gold pieces to be split between the two little sisters, for a very modest dowry, just enough to get them married and started on a life of their own.

Naomi cried. Her mother cried, too. In all Naomi's young girl dreams of what her life might be like, she had never dreamed anything like this.

Naomi took a deep breath, and wiped her eyes. Naomi knew that she and her family continually subsisted at the edge of starvation. As a slave of a wealthy brothel owner, at least she would be pretty sure of getting enough to eat. By this one choice, she could provide for her mother and two sisters more thoroughly than any other way in her whole life.

Naomi looked at her mother, and then squeezed her eyes shut, and nodded. The next day her mother sold her to the brothel owner.

By the time Naomi was 24, she had borne six children. Two of them probably were fathered by the slave-owner himself, the other four by random customers. All six of the babies had been sold by the slave-owner.

In nine years as a slave prostitute, Naomi had learned that it was important to be good at her job. If regular customers asked for her by name, the slave-owner would give her small rewards. If customers complained about her, she would be beaten. Naomi had learned that she must always appear happy and satisfied, no matter how she might feel in her soul.

How she felt in her soul was mostly dead.

Oh, there were times when her laughter was not entirely fake. Sometimes when she and some of the other girls were chatting late on a springtime morning, Naomi was surprised to discover that, at least for a few moments, she actually felt almost cheery.

During the seasons when food was sparse, reports would come in of those who had died of starvation — two or three from an outlying settlement, a dozen or so from a nearby village, sometimes tales of hundreds from a neighboring province. Naomi would acknowledge to herself that by now she surely would have been one of those who had slowly and painfully starved to death. In those moments she felt grateful that she always had enough to eat.

But mostly how Naomi felt in her soul was dead. She was 24 years old. She would be a slave there in the brothel for the rest of her life, as a prostitute for perhaps the next twenty years. Then they would turn her into a scrubwoman for whatever years were left to her. Then she would die. That would be her life.

Every once in a while, Naomi allowed herself a few moments to believe that it was worth it because her family had survived. They had not starved. Her mother's health was frail, Naomi had heard, but she was still getting by, and she had managed to preserve enough for small dowries for Naomi's two little sisters, now both happily married. She hoped they were grateful. She hoped they remembered her. But she also knew she was an embarrassment; no one wants to admit there's a harlot in the family.

Then she would force herself to put that topic firmly away, for if she allowed herself to dwell on the topic of family, she knew her tears would overwhelm her. Then she would not do her job well, and she would be beaten. So she would once again put on her cheery face over her deadened heart.

One night a boy came into the brothel. He looked like a young prince — all in fine clothes, leather boots with fancy buckles, a gold signet ring. He was about seventeen, wide-eyed, eager, and a little scared. He looked over the girls in the house, picked out Naomi, and paid the owner his money.

He returned the next evening, and quite often after that — sometimes with a bunch of his friends — sometimes by himself. When he brought his friends, there was always a party, paid for by the young prince, with wine and figs, cheese and honeycakes for everyone.

The gossip was all about this boy. Where had he come from? No one knew. Just that he had a royal amount of money, and he seemed to be trying to see how fast he could spend it all.

It took him a couple of months to spend it all.

During that time, the boy had become a regular customer, showing up in the evening, paying his money to the slave-owner, and taking Naomi off to one of the rooms for the night. He never said much, except to brag about how smart and rich he was. Naomi had long since learned how to appear quite fascinated when customers were full of big talk, so it took no effort to make her fake smile look dazzlingly real as she flattered this young boaster for all he claimed he had accomplished.

Then, in the middle of one very dark night, she awoke to discover he was trembling, and when she whispered his name, he blurted out that he didn't know what he was going to do. His inexhaustible supply of money was dwindling fast. He soon would have nothing left.

"What will you do?" she asked.

He didn't know. Finally, he said he would try to get a job. But it was completely the wrong time of year to find work, and they both knew it.

Naomi asked, "Can you go back to your family?" She didn't know why she asked that. It was not a question she wanted to ask, not a topic she wanted to talk about: *family* was a place Naomi knew she could never go.

Yet, the question hung there in the dark for a long time. The boy didn't say anything. Naomi didn't say anything. Finally she felt him shaking his head. "No," the boy said. "I can never go back. I would ..." and his voice broke with emotion.

Naomi supposed he was about to say why he couldn't go back home. She thought maybe he wanted her to ask again and draw an answer out of him, but she was afraid. Any further discussion about family was more than she could survive.

When the boy left the brothel in the grey light of early dawn, Naomi knew she would never see him again. He would do his best to hang onto whatever money he had left. But no — he showed up that evening, looking like he had not a care in the world. Except that his ring was gone. He showed up the following evening as well — and the next. Only Naomi knew of the fear in his soul, his silent weeping in the middle of the night. Sometimes he asked if she had heard anything about work he might do, or he would talk of the dreams he once had held and now had ruined. Naomi listened. She wondered why he could not go back to his family. She wanted to ask, but she did not dare, for talking about family would mean her own heartbreak would burst out and she would cry herself to death.

Then one night the boy did not show up.

One of the old women, Abigail, brought the gossip back from the market a few days later. The boy had gotten a job as a migrant worker on a pig farm. Everyone giggled over the irony of it — from prince to pig boy in just a couple of months. Naomi giggled with the others. She did not want the others to see the bitterness in her soul, so she put extra mocking into her giggle. She was so angry at herself for caring about this boy. He was just another trick, just another loser trying to be a man by buying a night with a woman. The conversations they had shared didn't mean a thing. He didn't mean a thing.

Some farmers who hired migrant workers made sure they got a hot meal and a spot in the bunkhouse, while waiting for their first payday, but the farmer who had hired their young prince was notable for his stinginess. People had sometimes commented about it, "Why don't you provide food for your workers?" He just shrugged, "I pay the standard wage. It's up to them to buy their own food. If they didn't save enough money from their previous job to buy food to last until payday, that's not my problem."

The gossipers enjoyed thinking that this farmer's stinginess meant that the boy who had been such a prince was now slopping hogs, watching the animals chow down while he himself had nothing to eat. What irony — what *delicious* irony! All the brothel girls laughed at that picture. Naomi joined right in. But she also remembered what hunger felt like. She remembered when she'd been twelve and thirteen and fourteen, all those times when for two days there was nothing to eat. Then those had become normal, and the hard times were when it had taken three or four days of scrounging, gleaning, searching, begging, always with this endless famished ache in your middle, until finally you got hold of some scraps to push the hunger back for a little while. Naomi knew what it meant to go hungry. She listened to the others laughing at the prince who became a pig boy. Naomi laughed, too, because not to laugh would be to admit she cared about that boy. She did not care, she insisted to herself. But she did remember what it felt like, to go hungry.

Gossip only stays juicy for a while. There was a brief note a week or so later, someone commented that the boy had apparently moved on; he was no longer working for that stingy farmer. Soon the routine of gossip turned to other topics, as it always does, and the boy was forgotten.

Then, a couple weeks later the story was all over town. Abby came back from the market with the news. This boy had indeed gone home to his family, and before he even made it in the door his father started barking out the orders to all the servants. They had thrown an enormous feast, because the old man was so glad to have his son back again.

They all started chattering away, quite impressed with such a story, but Abigail shushed them, because she had more to tell them. "*Well*," she said, "his *father* may have been happy to see him, but his older *brother* was quite steamed about the whole thing! And the father and the brother had an enormous glorious confrontation right in the doorway of the celebration. And you'll never guess what happened next! Just let me tell you...."

Once upon another time, there was a presbytery meeting. (In other denominations the churches within a given region are called a district or a diocese or a conference. In the Presbyterian tradition, to which I belong, we name such a collection — with remarkable creativity — a *presbytery*.) It had been a long day at the presbytery meeting, as the ministers and elders (ordained lay representatives from the churches of the presbytery) listened to more reports on more topics than we could count. Finally, we came to the highlight of the day; we went downstairs to eat dinner in the church's fellowship hall.

While everyone else got in line heading down the steps, I spent a few minutes chatting with a friend who was heading home early instead of staying for dinner and the evening part of the meeting. By the time we finished our conversation, I ended up last in line. People commented on that. They might have concluded, "Wow, he thinks so much of others, he let everyone else go ahead of him in line," but it seems nobody came to that conclusion. A number of them had seen me talking with my friend there on one side of the sanctuary while everyone else was going down to dinner, so they might have supposed, "He was so deep in spiritual conversation, food was no longer a consideration." Apparently nobody came to that conclusion, either.

Instead there were catcalls about how I must have gotten lost on the way downstairs, and amazement that I would ever end up at the tail end of the dinner line.

The church basement was full. Just about every seat at every table was already in use. I looked around to find a place to sit with my friends, but they were all at tables with no vacancies. I ended up finding a place at a table with half a dozen men I had never met.

There was already a conversation going on as I sat down. The elder sitting next to me was responding to the presentation on world hunger we'd had that afternoon, commenting — complaining, really — about the television program he had seen the other week. It was one of those programs that shows you all the children with anguished faces and distended bellies, with the 800-number flashing on the bottom of the screen, and you can phone in your credit card number to make a donation right then.

The man felt this kind of programming was bad. It was abusive, really, piping that into people's living rooms where they'd run into it while they were clicking through the channels to see what was on. He declared that it could hardly be an effective way of raising money to deal with the problem. Wouldn't most people just feel distressed and turned off by shows like that? He said he reckoned that if he sold off all his property and spent every nickel to buy food for those people, it wouldn't even begin to make a dent in the size of the problem.

I had some things I wanted to say to that, but my mouth was full, because the ladies of the church had done a great job on the meal. I was doing my Christian best to eat hearty, so there was a brief silence.

This turned out to be a good thing. (Often it is a good thing, when ministers pause for a moment of silence. It can give someone else a chance to say something. Sometimes the person who gets to speak during the silence is one of the other people at the table. Sometimes the person who gets to speak during the silence is God.)

On this occasion, the silence gave the man sitting across from me enough time to think about it for a few seconds, and then muster up his courage to say, "I agree that what you see on a show like that isn't pretty, but I disagree with the last part of what you said. You see, about six years ago my wife and I decided we wanted to try to respond with real dollars to real needs like that. We decided we'd give $100 a month. When we checked into it further, that turned out to be enough money to provide food, clothing, shelter, and education for ten children at an orphanage in India. On a percentage basis, you're right; it makes no difference in the size of the problem of world hunger. But it sure makes a difference for those ten children. Providing for the needs of ten kids may not change the world. But my wife and I believe it changes the world for those ten."

Once upon yet another time, there was a story, a story that Jesus used to tell, a story we usually call the "Parable of the Prodigal Son."[1] It is perhaps the best known of all Jesus' parables, but it raises some questions that remain unresolved to this very day. For example, as Luke has recorded the story, he's given it to us in a fairly terse style. Jesus may well have taken ten or twenty minutes to tell the story, and included many of the details his listeners would routinely want to know — like where did it happen and how old were the boys and what did their mother say about all this? And how much money was it, and what business was this family in, after all? And especially, why on earth did the father give in to the boy's request?

Yet, if Luke has given us less of the story than we would like, he still provided much more information than Matthew did (Matthew 21:28-30). This parallel gives us a story with two sons and a father, where one son rebels and later repents, while the other appears to be obedient, yet ends up estranged — very similar in framework, yet quite different in length. Has Matthew taken a longer version of the story and reduced it to a two-sentence summary of the boys' behavior, because he specifically wants to focus our attention on how the two sons moved in opposite directions?

Exercise 2-1

Read the following two passages out loud, twice each. You'll want to note how long it actually takes to complete each of the four readings.

1. Read Luke 15:11-32 with rapid-fire staccato excitement — on the basis that this story is so amazing that you want to get it all told as quickly as you can, so that everyone who is listening can find out how it goes.
2. Now read Luke 15:11-32 a second time, with deliberate pauses and considerable expression — on the basis that this story is so moving that you want everyone who is listening to have moments along the way to savor the deep emotional content given to us as the story unfolds.
3. Read Matthew 21:28-30 with rapid-fire staccato excitement — on the basis that this story is so fascinating that you want to get it all told as quickly as you can, so that everyone who is listening can find out how it goes.
4. Now read Matthew 21:28-30 a second time, with deliberate pauses and considerable expression — on the basis that this story is so moving that you want everyone who is listening to have moments along the way to savor the deep emotional content given to us as the story unfolds.

How long does the fastest version take? How long does the longest take? Suppose it took Jesus fifteen minutes or so to tell the original version of the story of the prodigal son, because he included many details that neither Luke nor Matthew has recorded because they were both in a hurry to tell the story more quickly. By what percentage might they have reduced the plot line?

It could well be, then, that both Matthew and Luke have given us seriously abbreviated versions of a story that Jesus told at greater length. Or it could be Jesus himself who took one basic story — the story of a father and his two sons who reversed their behaviors

— and told that story in different ways on different occasions: sometimes as briefly as Matthew has given it to us, on other occasions with the level of detail we find in Luke, and perhaps occasionally at much fuller length.[2]

Whichever of these possibilities seems the most plausible as an explanation of the texts of Matthew and Luke, we are left with the conclusion that the story doesn't have to be told the same way every time. Sometimes the story could be told in two sentences — make the contrast, and be done. Sometimes the story could be told at considerable length, with much more plot provided to draw the listener into the depth of the story.

If Jesus could feel that narrative freedom as he told stories to his followers, if Matthew and Luke could feel that narrative freedom as they wrote stories down for their readers, can preachers today feel that same narrative freedom as we recount stories to our congregations?

This sense of narrative freedom may well be the best explanation for the similarities and differences among the gospel accounts. It's the same story being told, from one passage to the next, but the storytellers felt comfortable telling it different ways.

For example, all four gospels record the story we usually call the feeding of the 5,000, but their accounts are not identical.[3] Matthew, Mark, and Luke report that the disciples urge Jesus to send the crowd away, so that the people can go buy themselves something to eat. In John, however, Jesus puts the disciples to the test, asking them where they will go to buy food for all the gathered crowd. Similarly, Matthew, Mark, and Luke give us the impression that the five loaves and two fish comprise all the food that the disciples have with them. In contrast John indicates that the five loaves and two fish are provided by an unnamed lad, apparently from among the multitude.

It is commonplace of New Testament studies that the first three gospels tell essentially the same story, while the fourth offers a marked contrast in style, content, emphasis, and detail. These two items — Who will buy the food for the multitude? and Where do the loaves and fish come from? — illustrate this well; the synoptics provide one answer, and John offers us another. Although the common pattern is for Matthew, Mark, and Luke to agree with each other and disagree with John, this is no hard and fast rule. Within this same story we find a couple of counterexamples. Thus we can see Mark and John in agreement on how the disciples worried that it would cost 200 denarii — perhaps eight months' wages for a laborer — to buy sufficient food to feed these people, while Matthew and Luke do not comment on the cost. Again, John and Matthew remark that the people sit down on the grass. Mark specifies that it is green grass while Luke makes no mention of the grass.

In another example, all four of the gospels record Palm Sunday, the entry into Jerusalem, with Jesus riding on a borrowed donkey, with great acclaim from the crowds (Matthew 21:1-11; Mark 11:1-10; Luke 19:29-40; John 12:12-15). Clearly, the synoptics parallel each other quite closely, while John's version is shorter and worded differently. But again, there are agreements that do not match this general principle. John and Matthew both cite the words from Zechariah 9:9, while Mark and Luke make no reference to the fulfillment of prophecy. Mark and Luke tell at length about how the disciples go to borrow a donkey, in contrast to John's single line indicating that Jesus got a donkey, but these three do at least agree that there was just one donkey. Matthew is the one with the contrasting testimony, as he goes to the trouble to show us the disciples fetching two donkeys, a mother and her colt, for Jesus to sit on and ride into Jerusalem.

Why are there these similarities and differences? They are similar because these storytellers were telling the same story. They are different because Matthew, Mark, Luke, and John felt quite comfortable telling the story in different ways, as they perceived would be most useful or moving for their audiences, without feeling that the stories required them to use exactly the same phrasing and emphasis every time.

Most studies of the Bible are not studies about stories about the narrative freedom of storytellers and their storytelling. Instead, most studies of the Bible are studies of the biblical documents. The recurring question has been, how did these documents come to be written? What earlier documents did they depend on, how did these various documents influence one another, which authors edited which sources and combined the results with what other material, in order to create the texts which have come down to us in the manuscript tradition?

This is important scientific work. All who read the Bible are indebted to the many scholars who have devoted lifetimes to provide their best understanding of the actual text of the Bible, the genres of literature it contains, the history of its compilation, and many similar details that help us come to our own best understanding of scripture and its message.

Yet, in the end, that kind of work is about documents, and while preachers should be grateful for all those who have worked to show what is in the documents, the stories and songs of scripture were alive before the words were put down in writing. The stories were told, the songs were sung, and they moved the hearts of listeners because God spoke to them through these words before the ink was ever on the parchment.

And storytellers and singers — and preachers — have always felt a great deal of narrative freedom, to put the words together in the way that they felt would be the most helpful, or moving, or clear.

Exercise 2-2
Take a few moments to remember a story from your early teen years, when you and a friend got into a certain amount of mischief together. You want one where you did something embarrassing, where you may have gotten into some amount of trouble, and learned a lesson that has enabled you to look at life a little differently. Tell that story, out loud, three times.

1. Tell the major story of that incident, including your friend's name, whose idea it was to take on the project, why it seemed like fun at the time, and how it backfired on you. Tell it as a joke on yourself, along the lines of "Let me tell you about this dumb thing we did." Your account might be a dozen to twenty sentences long.

2. Tell that story again, but this time as a very brief plot summary, with minimal details (almost as if it is awkward to admit to those details), no more than three sentences, two if you can.
3. The third time, offer a brief acknowledgment of the incident (one sentence or less), as minimal background on the way to telling the rest of the story, the lesson you learned from it, what happened next, how you looked at life somewhat differently from then on.

(If you have just read through to this point in the exercise without telling the story out loud, *stop and go back and do it. Really.*)

All three of these are legitimate editions of this story. None of them is a lie. But they are very different in length, content, and emphasis. Despite those differences, though, you could probably switch comfortably from one to another, depending on which one you thought would be most useful or interesting or moving, in a given setting.

Your grandchildren might find those switches to be considerably more challenging, however. Even if they have heard you tell the story different ways on different occasions, and even if it seemed quite natural to them at the time (that is, they easily recognized that you were giving a longer or briefer rendition of the same story), there may well be one version that they remember best — and that's the one they would probably write down, so that it would not be forgotten.

And their grandchildren, in turn, will read the story that way, and probably not even be aware that you told this story different ways, on different occasions.

Narrative freedom is the ordinary process where someone telling a story makes choices — what to put in, what to leave out, what to emphasize, what to downplay. Narrators exaggerate, stating their point with grand, sweeping images, so that the listeners not only understand but also feel the point that is being made. They compress and expand time, covering decades in a few seconds, or taking five minutes to describe all the feelings someone felt during the first few moments of falling in love. They feel the freedom to use whatever figures of speech seem most effective, in order to create a narrative that will help the hearers see and feel and know what is happening.

Once upon a time someone in the crowd said to Jesus, "Make my brother divide the inheritance with me." But Jesus didn't help the family work out a just and equitable settlement; instead, he made up a story about a man so rich he didn't know what to do, who had a conversation with God in a dream (Luke 12:13-21). On another occasion Jesus was talking about how important it was for his followers to root the sin out of their lives, he engaged in astonishingly vivid rhetoric, explaining the process as if people should cut off their hands and pluck out their eyes (Matthew 5:29-30; 18:8-9). When a law professor tried to debate with Jesus about who does and doesn't count as a neighbor, Jesus did not help devise a list of criteria as to who qualifies, but rather made up a story about how various people treated a man who had been beaten by robbers (Luke 10:25-37). When the scribes accused him of being demon-possessed, Jesus spun off a quick two-verse parable about someone who has to be stronger than a strong homeowner in order to plunder his household (Mark 3:22-27; Matthew 12:24-29; Luke 11:15-22).

Narrative freedom, then, follows the example of Jesus and the gospel writers. Nevertheless, even the idea of free narration within a sermon can make people quite uncomfortable. There are at least a couple of reasons for this. The first has to do with honesty. Narrative freedom could easily appear to be pretty much the same thing as lying. How can this be acceptable behavior for a preacher? Yet many preachers do engage in lying in their sermonizing. If I make up a story about something I have accomplished, or claim that an event I have heard from someone else actually happened to me, that almost certainly counts as lying. Yet telling the truth is not always acceptable, either. Most preachers know a lot of true stories that would provide excellent insights within our sermon, yet if we reveal the helpful and interesting details we have learned about the lives of the people of the congregation and community, that will be breach of confidentiality.

One level of narrative freedom takes place when preachers tell us, "This story is true, but I've changed some of the details to protect people's privacy." That may be a workable compromise, yet it does indeed have its risks. In many congregations there will be some people who will spend the rest of the service working out in their own minds who they think you're talking about, and will then spend the rest of the week spreading their guesses, right or wrong, to others. In any case, changing the details is clearly an instance of using narrative freedom in the effort to balance "telling the truth" and "keeping confidentiality."

Perhaps this differentiation will be helpful. Lies are brief statements or longer stories we make up that serve to get us out of trouble or to make ourselves look better than we are. The parables Jesus told were brief statements or longer stories he made up that served to illuminate the truth of the gospel. When we as preachers exercise narrative freedom, we don't get to tell lies, but we do get to follow the example of Jesus.

The second reason many of us feel uncomfortable with the idea of narrative freedom has to do with our preference for the familiar over the challenging. Those who preach and those who listen have a lot of personal experience with sermons that aim at building a systematic understanding of the faith. They may not be too lively, but at least they are pretty much what we were expecting. If I give you a list of ten reasons why you should read your Bible every morning, or an exposition of how it is that the death of someone twenty centuries ago can make an actual difference for people today, then (if I manage to keep you awake) you will find that your understanding is stronger than it was before.

A gain in understanding is not bad, but neither is it an encounter with God. If I do nothing more than tell the story of "Abraham and Isaac on Mount Moriah," or the story of "The Unjust Judge and the Persistent Widow" (Genesis 22:1-12; Luke 18:1-8), your heart will be moved. Moreover, it's likely you will be left wondering, "What does it mean? How am I supposed to understand this? Is this what God is like? How do I feel about that?" Suppose I retell these stories at length, utilizing the narrative freedom to place them within a contemporary setting — adding enough detail to create the same kind of context where you yourself have felt that God was at fault.

What's that? You want to object that whatever difficulties may arise, it cannot be the case that God is at fault? Well, preacher, haven't you yourself had times when God has ignored your heartfelt pleas for what is right? Haven't you yourself had times when God has made demands on you that were far too demanding — outrageous, contradictory, inescapably wrong — and yet they were the demands of God? You are not the only one who has had experiences like that. They are also part of the testimony of scripture, in stories like "Abraham and Isaac on Mount Moriah" and "The Unjust Judge and the Persistent Widow."

Suppose, then, I tell one of these stories, so that you can recognize that this is your story, too? Just like in the old complaint about the minister who had left preaching and gone on to meddling, a narrative sermon like that could easily push you beyond your own comfort level. Instead of offering the familiar and expected exposition of a Bible passage, it puts you in the uncomfortable story of someone experiencing a difficult encounter with God. The more you identify with the story, the more uncomfortable it will make you feel — and nobody likes feeling uncomfortable. Yet, that discomfort is also an invitation to encounter God. It puts you in the midst of your own feelings regarding your similar troubling situation — a place where you might well encounter God.

There is no guarantee that that will happen. You might simply not get it, and therefore conclude that the sermon doesn't have much of a point this morning. Or you might lament that you wish the preacher would simply explain the passage and move on to the closing hymn.

And yet maybe, just maybe, you will hear the voice of God in the midst of that retelling of the story, in a way that would not happen, in the sermons about ten reasons for reading your Bible or how to understand the atonement. As I tell a story about God interacting with other people, perhaps that will be the moment that you will hear God speaking to you.

That's why the biblical authors wrote the Bible the way they did. They wrote the Bible in the hope that people would encounter

God, through the stories and songs they recorded there. That's why preachers preach — in the hope that people will encounter the presence of God.

Exercise 2-3

All four gospels record the last supper that Jesus shared with his disciples; yet they do this in greatly contrasting ways. All four recount the crucifixion and resurrection, with even greater variations.

Read the following four passages out loud. Read them simply and slowly, letting yourself hear each of them as its own story.

1. Matthew 26:17—28:20
2. Mark 14:12—16:8
3. Luke 22:7—24:53
4. John 6:53-59; 13:1-7; 18:1—21:25

There are remarkable contrasts in the way the four evangelists told this part of the story of Jesus. Throughout all four of the gospels, they recounted the same incidents with striking similarities. Then we come to the story of this meal. In their differing ways, all four indicated that this meal Jesus shared with his disciples stands as an event of great importance for understanding what the Jesus story is all about. We come to the climax of the narrative, Jesus' crucifixion and resurrection. Again, all four made it clear that these events are of the very essence of Christian belief. We encounter astonishing variety, as we read of the last supper, the crucifixion, and the resurrection, for the gospel writers told about these events by talking about different people, in different places, having different conversations. It is difficult to argue that they were concerned to record these critical matters by following one specified pattern — let alone following one specified wording.

Imagine that a member of the church youth group, a high school senior, has come to you, asking about these contrasts, quite concerned because it appears that the Bible is providing contradictory information here, not with regard to some obscure doctrine, but with regard to the very heart of the Christian faith. Use what you know about narrative freedom to explain to this student that the contrasts in the account are not like contradictions in a law court or in a philosophy text, but are instead like the way that people tell stories about key parts of the family history at a family reunion, sometimes briefly, sometimes at length, sometimes recalling one incident told from one person's point of view, sometimes sharing how it looked from someone else's perspective.

When Luke recorded "The Parable of the Prodigal Son, the Astonishingly Generous Father, and the Angry Older Brother" for us, there's another key feature that we must not miss — namely, the story stops before it gets to the end. Jesus told the story up to the point where we see the father and the older brother standing there toe-to-toe at the threshold of the great celebration. The hardworking, faithful son is raging on the doorstep and his father is pleading with him to come in and welcome his brother home. Then Jesus stopped the story, right there. It is an impossible place for the story to stop. We need to know what happens next. But Jesus stopped the story right there, and did not tell us how the story would end.

What does that mean? It means that Jesus has left it up to us to figure out how the end of the story goes. Giving us the narrative freedom to finish the story makes it possible for us to come up with more than one ending. We will have to decide what to do about that.

"The Parable of the Prodigal Son" is a story about grace. It is a story about the grace of God, wherein we discover that when God is in the story there is no predicting how wild the story may become. The grace that comes from God is not tame; instead, it is astonishing.

The tale begins with a boy who has calmly wished his father dead: "I don't want to live in your household, Dad, I just want the money I'll inherit from you when you die." Then the boy goes out and ruins his life. After he has gone hungry for a while, he considers that he would at least get to eat every day if his old man would consent to give him a job as a laborer on the farm. Even that is surely more than the brat deserves. Yet, the astonishing love of his father is this: He welcomes the boy back as a beloved son.

"The Parable of the Prodigal Son" is also a story about the struggle we have putting the grace of God into practice. The older brother feels a deep resentment in his soul — a grudge that anyone can sympathize with. He has endeavored to be faithful. Perhaps his attitude has been surly from time to time. Perhaps he has been more dutiful and less cheery than he ought to have been. But isn't that small potatoes, compared to the inescapable fact that he has been there? He has been there, doing his duty — reliable and faithful. Doesn't that count for anything?

The prodigal comes dragging back. Possibly he is genuinely repentant, possibly he is merely very hungry, hoping to get a menial job that includes supper every night. With astonishing graciousness and joy, the father welcomes him and restores him to full sonship once more. The older brother has neither graciousness nor joy; he has rage. But the father expects his older son to respond with graciousness and joy.

How big is the grace of God? Is it big enough to welcome the prodigal home? Apparently so. The story has shown us that welcome. Is the grace of God big enough to transform the heart of the older brother? Jesus has stopped telling the story. As we tell — and live — the story, it is up to us to decide how the story will proceed from here.

Suppose the older brother stalks off into the darkness, perhaps in sullen silence, perhaps with angry curses. It would certainly be understandable if he does that. But what does that mean? What does it mean if the sinners come home to live in the presence of God, and those who have endeavored to be faithful decide they cannot accept that, and so they choose to turn away from God and head out into the darkness? If we can ruin our relationship with the Father through promiscuous sinfulness, can we also ruin our relationship with the Father through self-righteous sinfulness? If the Father longs for the return of the prodigal, how will the Father feel about the departure of the faithful brother? Will there be a time of bitterness for the older, faithful brother? Will he eventually see that he can end up lost in his bitterness, just like his brother was lost in his libertinism? Despite the father's longing, the prodigal son was dead and gone forever; he could never return home to his father as long as he stayed far away, lost in his despair. Is the same true for the bitter son, then? Despite the Father's longing, will the bitter son be just as dead and gone forever, never able to return home to his father as long as he stays out in the darkness, lost in his rage?

I expect that these are not theoretical questions for some of the people you know, preacher. It is not obvious how they should be answered. Yet in order for you to finish telling the story, you must decide how you will answer these questions.

How big is the grace of God? If the grace of God is big enough to forgive the prodigal brother, is the grace of God also big enough to transform the heart of the bitter brother?

Perhaps the story continues like this: The older son turned sharply away from his father, and fled in anger into the darkness. His father took two steps to follow him and then stopped at the edge of the porch. Perhaps he could have caught up, but he knew that once your children reach a certain age, they do what they do. If they won't listen, you cannot make them listen. He shook his head, asking himself, "Is this the way it always will be? As soon as you start to get one back on track, the other one immediately goes off the rails." And he felt the immense longing within him for his older son, just like he had felt it when his younger son had left.

But the older brother knew nothing of this, as he ran deeper into the dark night, with tears burning his face. A few hundred yards from the house, he tripped and fell over a tree root, skidding headlong in the dirt. It hurt. Not as much as the ache in his heart, though. So he just lay there on the ground, blood oozing from his scrapes and mixing with the dust and the tears to form a sticky mud on his cheek. He didn't care. He thought, "Fine, I'll just go off and squander the family money on liquor and whores, too, and then my father will love me like he does that brat."

He stayed out in the dark for a long time. Perhaps it was through all the long hours of that one night. Perhaps it was longer. The bile in his soul made it feel like years. Perhaps it really was years. Lost in his bitterness, time passed, with the joy gone from his heart forever. Forever? Perhaps it really was forever. Perhaps that aching sense of betrayal he felt because it was so unfair — so unfair — *so unfair* for his father to welcome back that horrible faithless delinquent — perhaps that sense of betrayal ran so deep that he never ever overcame it, so he stayed out in the dark, away from his father's presence, forever.

When Jesus stopped talking before he got to the end of the story, was that the way he intended for us to tell what happened next? Maybe it is.

But maybe not. Perhaps, instead, the story continues like this.

The older son turned sharply away from his father. He wanted to run screaming into the darkness. He wanted to curse his father in the foulest language he could find. He wanted to march into that party, punch his ugly brother square on the nose, and then grab him by the neck and drown him in the punchbowl.

But he did none of those things. Instead, he took a deep breath. He turned back to his father, and nodded. He walked in to the celebration. To the depths of his soul he felt the rage, but he allowed none of it to show — or almost none. Somehow he could not muster up quite enough enthusiasm to make it seem that he really was happy to see his long-lost brother. His words of greeting were clipped. Brief. Terse. And yet, correct. He said all the right things.

Despite his effort to make sure that nothing in his words or his tone or his face would reveal his bitterness, some of it still leaked through, as he bade his brother welcome home. The younger son was not fooled. He sensed the bile simmering in his older brother's heart and knew that it would erupt some day.

But it did not erupt that day. Everyone felt the tension in the room, as they did their best to be festive and glad. The musicians played their happy songs. The waiters served all the special food prepared for the banquet. The guests laughed and sang, and stood up and offered impressive toasts, with clinking glasses filled with sparkling wine. It was almost a great celebration. But everyone felt the tension of fury-kept-in-check, and knew that it would rage forth some day.

One week passed. Another. Month by month, the two brothers lived together with a constant tense undercurrent, with the awareness on both their parts that there was a great painful chasm between them that would always be there. There was nothing the younger brother could say or do to make it go away. There was nothing the older brother could say or do to make it go away. Just an enduring learn-to-live-with-it pain, like an aching tooth with no dentist to fix it. They lived out the rest of their lives with aching souls, with no one to fix it. They did not live happily ever after. Instead, they lived in quiet, bitter tension, ever after.

When Jesus stopped talking before he got to the end of the story, was that the way he intended for us to tell what happened next? Maybe it is.

As I noted, preacher, it is likely that you know people whose lives tell this story, in one or the other of these two ways, as rage that has led to long separation, or as bitterness that has led to strained despair. Indeed there may be quite a few of them gathering this Sunday morning in hopes that God might somehow touch the pain within their hearts.

How might the Word of God speak to them, if you were to tell once again the story of the prodigal son, and included this part of the story?

Year by year, the two brothers lived next door to each other, with this great unresolved ache. On the surface, life seemed acceptable — the business was making money, the children were doing well in school. There were rumors of wars far away, but no crime in the neighborhood. Things were going well at church. Both brothers had been elected elders. One served on the property committee and tried to figure out how to bring the wiring up to code. The other taught Sunday school for the junior high class.

Then came the month where both were appointed to go to the presbytery meeting. That's pretty unusual, but sometimes unusual things happen. When I came down the stairs, got my plate, and found my seat at the table there, with these people I had never met before, I didn't realize that two of those elders were brothers from the same church. They were not sitting next to each other; instead, they were at opposite ends of the table, and neither of them said a word, as we listened to the exchange between the man who hated feed-the-hungry infomercials and the man who had decided, along with his wife, to change the world for ten orphans.

The prodigal brother and the bitter brother drove home from the presbytery meeting later that evening. Neither of them mentioned the interchange between those other two men at dinner. Neither of them mentioned me, either, but there was no reason to mention me. Even though I was the only ordained minister at the table, I hadn't said much of anything during the meal.

That's pretty unusual for me.

There are plenty of things I could say about the problem of world hunger. But in that particular moment, I was too busy eating to talk about feeding the poor.

It was in one of those quiet moments, in the midst of an empty space in the conversation that the preacher did not fill; that was when God spoke.

God spoke to the prodigal brother and to the bitter brother.

Who can say what it will be like, when God speaks to someone's heart? Will there be audible words? Will there be sentences and paragraphs? Will there be impressions, longings, convictions? When two people are listening to the same God, speaking to them both at the same time, will they hear the same command?

The two brothers had heard the same conversation, after all, between the man who was angry about give-to-feed-the-hungry programming and the man who supported ten orphans. Yet the two brothers did not hear God saying the same thing to them, around the edges of that conversation.

For the bitter brother, it was something like seeing a vision. He saw the angry man and the generous man, and God prompted his soul with the question, "What if the angry man were transformed to become a generous man, too?" And for just a moment, he saw what it could be like, if the soul of that man were transformed from his anger. He saw what God might do, in changing the world, if the energy of that man's anger were channeled into compassion. And for just a moment, he thought about his own bitterness. He saw the briefest of glimpses of what it would be like if God worked that same transformation in him. That was scary. He didn't know if he could handle that. He sat at the table, in silence, with his soul pondering on the vision of how the grace of God could transform the anger of the angry man into deep compassion and on how the grace of God might transform his own life, as well. And he said not a word. Not then, and not in the car on the way home.

But it was different for the prodigal brother. He had heard the man at supper comment that providing for the needs of ten children might not change the world, but it sure changed the world for those ten. And he heard the voice of God whisper in his soul, "You, too, could change the world. Just like that." And he thought, I can't even get real reconciliation to happen with my own brother, and I'm supposed to change the world for somebody? He tried to dismiss the idea, but that prompting was stubborn, "You could change the world like that." For a moment he wondered what it would be like, if he followed that voice and discovered that he really could change the world like that. What if he actually did make that kind of difference, in someone's life? It was so powerful that he almost spoke up and asked the man whose family supported ten orphans, "Do you happen to remember the 800 number or the name of the website where I could get in touch and check out that orphanage?" It was scary, and in the end, he said not a word about it. Not then, and not in the car on the way home.

Sometimes God speaks, and even though you know you can't prove it, your soul recognizes that it's the voice of God, whispering to you. But either by hesitation or stubbornness, you manage to put it out of your thoughts, and pretty soon you don't hear it any more. The two brothers rode home in silence. Neither of them knew how God had spoken to the other. They might well have been curious to hear about that, yet at the moment, each of them could still hear in their own soul the quiet echo of the voice of God, from that conversation at dinner. But either by hesitation or stubbornness, they managed to put the voice of God out of their thoughts, and pretty soon they did not hear it any more.

Nevertheless, God did not go away.

It was three or four days later, and the bitter brother was watching television. A commercial for kitchen cutlery came on. They flashed the 800 number — call now! And the bitter brother flashed back to that conversation at dinner, where the man had complained about hunger programs and their 800 numbers, and then he flashed once again to the vision God had given him of how that man's life could be transformed. He wondered once again whether the grace of God was big enough to transform the grudge in his life that he could not let go of.

A couple of weeks after that, the prodigal brother was sitting in the kitchen, feeling bored. There was a bowl of bread dough on the counter, covered with a damp cloth, slowly rising. It would be bread for supper that night. It raised in him a recollection of supper that night at the presbytery meeting, and how the voice of God had whispered in his soul that he could change the world. He stared at that bowl of bread dough, and he thought about how just a little yeast, mixed in with all that dough, leavens the whole lump. Such a small ingredient, to make such a large change. He remembered how Jesus said the kingdom of heaven is like a teaspoon of yeast transforming three gallons of bread dough. He thought to himself that if Jesus was right about that, then maybe the decisions of one individual could change the world for someone in need. He heard the voice of the Spirit whisper, "Yes!" in his soul, and even though he was not sure he had meant to ask a question, he smiled at the answer.

A few weeks after that, the prodigal son asked for a family meeting. Everyone gathered. His father and mother and grandmother. His older brother, along with his wife and their children. His three sisters and their families. A bunch of aunts and uncles, and dozens of cousins. They sat around six big tables in the great hall, with roast lamb, stuffing and gravy, new peas and mashed potatoes, corn bread and wheat bread and piping hot, dark rye dinner rolls, three bean salad and apple walnut salad. When they got together for a family meeting, it was always a feast.

The prodigal son stood up and began to make a speech. He said, "How big is the grace of God? Part of the story of my life is about discovering that it is very big. I found out that the grace of God does not want anyone to be left out. Because once upon a time, when I found myself out in the cold, hungry and alone, I learned that the grace of God is big enough to welcome home a prodigal son."

He looked at his father and mother, and smiled. His father and mother smiled back. He looked at his older brother, and smiled. To his surprise, his brother smiled back, too.

The older brother said, "I know that this is your speech, but I'd like to interrupt for a moment, if I may. It's a little embarrassing, to talk this way, but I need to try to say it anyway. Because I, too, have seen that the grace of God is very big. I, too, have discovered that God does not want anyone to be left out. Because I, too, have left myself out — outside the life of grace and joy that God intends for us all. I don't want it to be that way any more. I want us to be brothers once again."

The two brothers looked at each other. Neither moved. Then they both leaped. They leaped into each other's arms, they leaped across the room to hug one another with a fierce bear hug of brotherhood restored, with a grip that would never let go again — a grip that looked a lot like the fierce and irrepressible love of our God, so determined to leave no one out, so insistent on establishing grace and joy and restoration for all the prodigal sons and all the bitter brothers the world has ever known.

That's almost the end of the story.

But the prodigal son was not yet quite done with his speech. His speech had been upstaged a little, by this particular incident of the grace of God, and he didn't really mind, under the circumstances. Even so, he was determined to have the rest of his say.

Because God still wasn't done.

God still didn't want anyone to be left out.

The prodigal son said, "When I had come to the end of my resources, when I had run out of hope, there came a moment when God spoke to me. I didn't know at the time that the message came from God. It took me a little while to listen, but finally I did. God suggested that I should go home to my family. I didn't think I could. I thought I had ruined that possibility forever. So, I didn't listen for a while. Then I finally did listen. It was only when I listened to the voice of God, and came on home, that I discovered that the grace of God was big enough to welcome the prodigal home."

He paused for a moment, and then he said, "I might not have listened. Sometimes I catch myself wondering about what would have happened, if I had not listened. I probably would have starved to death by now."

All of the family looked around at the leftover food on the tables. They were all pretty well stuffed, and they could still see enough food left on the table for a full meal for them all. So it took some effort to contemplate what it might feel like, to starve to death.

The prodigal son said, "It was a slave girl. Her name was Naomi. She was a slave girl in a brothel, who spoke up and said the words that God would use to bring me home. This girl, Naomi, who had been sold into slavery, was the one who pointed me back to my family. She has no family. She has no future. She has no hope. But she said the words, the words that God used to redeem me, and to give me a family and a future and a hope once again. So I want to do something about that. It will cost some money, which is why I've asked for this family meeting. I want us to pay the cost of redeeming her, buying her away from her slave-owner."

The older brother said, "You want to use our family's money to buy a slave?"

The younger brother said, "I want to use some of our family's money to redeem a slave, yes. Why not? We've got the money. We can do this."

The older brother said, "You're serious? You plan to bring a prostitute home and make her part of our family?"

The younger brother shrugged. "I guess I could point out that eventually it worked out okay for Hosea. I might also suggest that Rahab, Tamar, and Bathsheba are all listed as part of the family of the Lord. I'm not even going to mention what Jesus said about it, immediately after he told our story, in Matthew 21:31-32. Nor will I bring up the reason he told the parable of the creditor with two debtors, at the home of Simon the Pharisee, in Luke 7:36-50.

"But no, bringing Naomi here to live with us is not really my plan. I expect that most of all she will want to go and connect back up with her own family, since I imagine she has not been able to see them for many years. But in any case, where she goes would be up to her. She'd be free to make her own decision, about this or anything else."

The older brother felt the rage starting to rise within him. First this horrible brother of his goes out and wastes half the family fortune sleeping with whores; now he wants to spend the other half redeeming them all. It made the older brother so mad, he felt like he could bite the head off a railroad spike. But since there were no railroad spikes available in the banquet room, he would just bite his brother's head off instead. As to that wondrous reconciliation he had just found with his brother, he could feel it slipping away. In his growing anger, he thought maybe he just didn't care if that reconciliation died before it was ten minutes old.

The prodigal son looked at his older brother and said, "You and I, my brother, have discovered that God doesn't want anyone to be left out. But we all manage to get ourselves left out, we get ourselves trapped in one kind of slavery or another, and we need to be redeemed. I was trapped in one kind of bondage. You were trapped in another kind of bondage. But God wants us all to be redeemed, so that none of us will have to stay trapped in whatever bondage we've ended up in. And you never know whom God might use, to help make it come true. Sometimes it's slave girls — but I think maybe this time it's us."

And it was just then that the older brother heard in his soul an echo from supper at that presbytery meeting, a few weeks earlier as the Spirit of holiness whispered to him, "Redeeming one person from slavery may not change the world. But it sure will change the world for that one."

Even then, the older brother did not say a word. He sat there in silence, for a long moment. The future hung in the balance, during that silence. The story could go in radically different ways, depending on what the older brother said next. He felt it — he felt the immense possibility of choosing a different future, he felt the power of the grace of God in that moment insisting that he did not have to remain stuck in his rage. But the rage was strong. He was not ready to let go of it. All the possibility of redemption was right there, for all the world and for his own soul, waiting for him to speak. The future hung in the balance. The world would turn out to be one way, or another, depending on what he said. But the rage was strong. He said not a word.

The future often hangs in the balance that way, doesn't it? The story could go in radically different ways, and indeed has done so — in your own experience, and in the lives of people in your church. The story sometimes has hung in the balance and then became one of miraculous redemption, and sometimes has hung in the balance and then fallen back into the same old pattern of despair. Which way will it go this time?

This chapter has been about the preacher and narrative freedom. I've provided some exegetical reasons for thinking that the stories within the Bible were told with a very large degree of narrative freedom, and that therefore we who retell Bible stories might well do the same. That could be an uncomfortable realization. But there it is, in the text, in the narrative freedom that Jesus and the gospel writers expressed, as they told the gospel story. I invite you to consider how you can go and do likewise, as you tell the gospel story.

I've also told you (most of) the story about "The Astonishingly Generous Father and his Two Sons Touched by Grace," a story that you thought you knew pretty well. Perhaps you have learned some new things about it, and about yourself, and about how you hear the voice of God, and about the places where it is hard for you to respond.

If that did indeed happen for you, did it mostly happen in the midst of the exegesis? Or during the telling and hearing of the story?

If a lot of your own discovery took place during the telling and hearing of the story, what does that suggest for your own preaching?

Of course, it *doesn't* mean you have to choose between exegesis and storytelling, as if from now on, either you can tell Bible stories but never again explain a Bible passage, or else you can explain Bible passages but never again tell a Bible story. After all, I went ahead and included both in this chapter, and you can include both in this Sunday's sermon.

As you consider the moments in the lives of your parishioners, when it is their stories that hang in the balance, it is worth asking yourself about where you think the discoveries you have made will be most likely to happen for them. Will it be as they come to understand a Bible passage, or as they find themselves involved in the narrative of a Bible story, that they will most readily hear the prompting of the Holy Spirit whispering to them? Will it be during the explanation or the storyline, do you think, that their hearts will find the faith and courage to say, "Yes," to God's call?

That may mean, preacher, that you need to find your way into the narrative freedom to tell some of those Bible stories in ways that your congregation has never heard before. When you do, perhaps they will hear them for the very first time. Best of all, perhaps they will hear the voice of God, speaking to them from the midst of the narrative.

Oh, and one more thing.

The older brother pushed back his chair. He stood up, slowly and deliberately. He looked at his younger brother. He looked around at all of the family gathered there. He looked back at his brother once more. And then he spoke. He said, "I believe it, my brother," and as he said it, he really did believe it, and he laughed a laugh of great and powerful joy. Then he said it again, and he said it loud: "I believe it, my brother!" Then he took another deep breath, and he said, "I believe God really does intend to redeem us all. You have learned that and I have learned that — even though I almost unlearned it, twenty seconds ago. You're right, sometimes it will indeed be people like us that God will use to make it happen. Maybe now it is, indeed, our turn. If we can change the world for one person, let's believe in God enough to go ahead and do it."

And they did.

Exercise 2-4

Among other things that have happened in this chapter, various aspects of the parable of the prodigal son have been recounted from shifting perspectives: from the point of view of a young girl sold into slavery, a man watching television, and a minister observing a conversation at a church dinner.

Choose one of the following shifts in perspective. Take ten minutes to tell the story, making it up right now as you go along.

1. "The Parable of the Prodigal Son," told from the perspective of the mother.
2. "The Parable of the Prodigal Son," told from the perspective of the servant who breaks the news to the older brother.
3. "The Parable of the Good Samaritan," told from the perspective of the Levite.
4. "The Parable of the Good Samaritan," told from the perspective of the lawyer.
5. "The Parable of the Good Samaritan," told from the perspective of a grandmother driving home alone Monday evening; she has just taught this lesson to her adult Sunday school class the previous morning, and now in the dusk she sees a woman standing next to a disabled car on the side of an empty stretch of highway.
6. "The Story of Zacchaeus," told from the perspective of Mrs. Zacchaeus.
7. "The Story of Zacchaeus," told from the perspective of a first-century person worrying about an upcoming tax audit.
8. "The Story of Zacchaeus," told from the perspective of a twenty-first-century person worrying about an upcoming tax audit.

---

1. Other names are certainly possible. Although many Bible editions have inserted a title in the margin or even within the main body of the text itself, the manuscripts of Luke 15:11-32 provide no name for the story. That leaves it up to us to come up with the best title. Consider how differently people might think about this passage if we ordinarily called it by another name. Suppose we knew it as "The Parable of the Angry Brother"? How about "The Parable of the Generous Father"? Perhaps it should be "The Parable of the Astonishingly Generous Father," or even "The Parable of the Ridiculously Generous

Father": What difference would that make in the way we "know" this story? Or what if we called it "The Story of Two Brothers Transformed from Greediness to Gratitude"?

2. Clarence Jordan has proposed one possibility for the larger story: Perhaps the younger brother became the Gerasene demoniac (Luke 8:26-39 and its parallels, Mark 5:1-20 and Matthew 8:28-34). The narrative of the healing takes place in a foreign country (Luke 8:26; 15:13), near where pigs were grazing in the fields (Luke 8:32; 15:15). It tells of one who returned to his senses (Luke 8:35; 15:17) and it concludes with the man going home to his family (Luke 8:39; 15:20). This is not nearly enough evidence to claim that we know that this connection is a fact. Even so, Jordan has given us a plausible speculation regarding an extensive piece of the story not included by Luke within the parable itself. *The Substance of Faith* (New York: Association Press, 1972), pp. 35-37.

3. Matthew 14:13-21; Mark 6:32-44; Luke 9:10-17; John 6:1-13. We would probably be better served to call this story the feeding of the 5,000 families. The enumeration is of 5,000 heads of household, plus their wives and children.

Chapter 3

Love Songs And Love Stories

preaching psalms of praise as a story

> *I wanted the woman, body and soul, as badly as I had ever wanted anything in all my life.*
>
> *I had entered Dufficy's Irish Store on Michigan Avenue to buy a present for my daughter, Jean, a student at Stanford, who was going to Ireland for the summer.*
>
> *The woman and I had exchanged a few words, a couple of quickly averted glances. I could hardly remember what she looked like when I stumbled out of the store.*
>
> *Yet she was my destiny. I knew it. So, it seemed, did she.*
>
> *The image of her body, pliant and happy under mine, hit me as I was leaving the store. I must have her. I, Brendan Ryan, the quietest of quiet men, had made up my mind.*
>
> *I must have her. I would have her.*
>
> *Soon.*[1]

Thus Andrew Greeley begins one of his many novels that use passionate human love as an analogue for the love of God. Many of us would find this idea awkward or even sinful. Yet Greeley is only one of many in a long line of Christians to offer this comparison. Ancient Christian commentators on the biblical Song of Solomon, for example — including such luminaries as Origen, Jerome, Athanasius, and Augustine — understood the book's erotic poetry in just this way. The sexual passion of the lovers, they thought, is an allegory of God's love for humanity, and our devoted response.

Why did they think that? It's easy enough to scoff that they probably interpreted the erotic imagery of the Song of Solomon as religious because they felt too uncomfortable with it as simply erotic.[2] These pages of scripture reveal a naked delight in sexual beauty and pleasure, but perhaps these men of the early church felt too embarrassed to deal with that, and so they spiritualized it away.

On the other hand, they may have been right, and Greeley and other modern writers may be right. Falling passionately in love with someone, complete with the eager longing of sexual arousal, the building toward climax, and the satisfaction of fulfillment — that kind of intensity may be one of the very best analogies of what the love between God and humanity is about.[3]

Still. As a preacher, can you actually *say* that? There are a couple of points that might well get you to hesitate here, and the first is this. If your sermon talks about erotic longing and fulfillment, will that successfully provide us with a strong analogy for God's love for us and our love for God? Or will it just get us thinking (again) about sex? Jesus described the people of his first-century world as an adulterous and sinful generation (Matthew 12:39; 16:4; Mark 8:38). Presumably he meant that they thought about sex a lot, and often the direction of these sexual thoughts was not covenantal. It would be hard to argue that our present generation doesn't have the same problem. The message the world declares in our day is that life is all about personal pleasure, quite apart from responsibility, covenant, or God. If you attempt to use passionate human longing as an analogue for our love for God, there is a substantial risk that our thoughts will not make the move from the first term of the analogy to the second.

The second reason for hesitating is that we might not be sure whether we really think it is true. Can religious passion be just as strong, just as compelling, just as good and fun and wondrous, as sexual passion? A lot of religious experience would say, "No." Moments of spiritual insight and moments of connection with God's love may be very fine things, but they will frankly not be as exciting as the physical experience of loving another human being.

If sexual excitement is ordinarily quite a bit more arousing than spiritual excitement could ever hope to be, then we might well hesitate over this analogy, despite the various ancient and modern writers who have utilized it because our analogy will end up promising more than it can actually deliver.

Consider, then — do we want to say, theologically, that a full and genuine encounter with God would have to be more moving and powerful than any sexual encounter? Or do we want to say that an encounter with God is noble and virtuous, even if it is not so exciting, and we should want such noble and virtuous encounters more than we want anything else? More than anything else, no matter how exciting that anything else might be? Simply because it is good, and goodness is better than pleasure?

As it turns out, the way you preach from the psalms will be significantly affected by the way you answer this question. That's why I've brought the subject up in this chapter. Still, more than preaching from the psalms is at stake here. This question has to do with the nature of God and with the essence and experience of salvation. It affects your life as a herald of the gospel, and your life as a Christian. You need to know the answer to this question, preacher.

Let me state it again, quite directly. When we gather to offer our hearts in worship to Almighty God, should that be exciting? As exciting as an action thriller, as exciting as an amusement park, as exciting as a football game, as exciting as sex?

Let's not just settle for your first quick off-the-cuff answer here. To help probe the question a bit, consider four characteristics that make things exciting.

1. **Strong emotional involvement**. It's more exciting when something is happening that touches me personally and gets my adrenaline pumping. Whether that is a roller coaster or a movie, it is important that I feel like I have become part of this thing, and how it comes out matters to me.
2. **Astonishment and wonder**. It's more exciting when I can't predict exactly what's going to happen next, when the things that happen catch me off guard.
3. **Gladness and celebration**. It's more exciting when there is a happy ending, when the good guys win, when the resolution is satisfying.

4. **Interpersonal communion**. It's more exciting when I'm not doing this alone, when there is someone else to share this with.

You can see how all four of these characteristics apply to these exciting-yet-very-different activities: a movie, a theme park, a football game, or a sexual experience.

Can these characteristics apply equally well to what the congregation does, in its encounter with God during worship on Sunday morning? That is: *When we gather to offer our hearts in worship to almighty God, should that be exciting?*

Wait, wait, people sometimes object right about here. Worship isn't supposed to be about fun or entertainment, they insist. When preachers put together the Sunday morning service with the aim of creating a show that will keep the congregation all jolly, they have missed the point of worship.

The objection makes an important point (one I fully agree with), yet it doesn't address the issue at hand. The question we need to answer is not, "Should we turn the Sunday morning service into a thrilling entertainment?" Rather, it is, "Is worshiping God an inherently thrilling thing to do?"

It's a legitimate question. If you feel that the proper answer is, "No, when God invented worship, it was never intended to be such an exciting thing," then you are perfectly free to make that response. If you feel the proper answer is, "Worship should be as exciting as any human endeavor you can name," then you are perfectly free to make that response.

In the following exercise, I invite you to reflect on the theological implications that arise from this question: *When we gather to offer our hearts in worship to Almighty God, should that be exciting?* With your own intuition you may have already answered that question, but for the purpose of the exercise, I encourage you to give serious consideration to both possibilities.

Exercise 3-1

Suppose we answer, "No." Coming into the presence of God is not supposed to be as exciting as various other activities. Write a sentence about what that implies for the following four items. For example, if the forgiveness of sins is not an exciting notion, what does that imply for your Christian life, and the life of the church?

Forgiveness of sins _____
_____
_____

Prayer _____
_____
_____

Church music _____
_____
_____

Discipleship _____
_____
_____

Suppose we answer, "Yes." Coming into the presence of God is supposed to be as exciting as various other activities. Again, write a sentence about what that implies for each of these four items. For example, if the forgiveness of sins is a very exciting notion, what does that imply for your Christian life, and the life of the church?

Forgiveness of sins _____
_____
_____

Prayer _____
_____
_____

Church music _____
_____
_____

Discipleship _____
_____
_____

It is possible to convey a great deal of excitement in just a few minutes, as many popular singers have demonstrated, if you put together evocative lyrics with a catchy rhythm and some upbeat instrumentation, and then deliver it with all you've got.

This is not a new discovery, however. They knew this back in Bible times. They picked many songs for inclusion within the canon of scripture because those songs expressed great excitement in worshiping God.

> *Praise the Lord!*
> *Praise God in his sanctuary; praise him in his mighty firmament!*
> *Praise him for his mighty deeds; praise him according to his surpassing greatness!*
> *Praise him with trumpet sound; praise him with lute and harp!*
> *Praise him with tambourine and dance; praise him with strings and pipe!*
> *Praise him with clanging cymbals; praise him with loud clashing cymbals!*
> *Let everything that breathes praise the Lord!*
> *Praise the Lord!* — Psalm 150

This psalm rocks with fervor, as the vocalists sing of God's surpassing greatness, with guitars and trumpets and pipes (piccolos? bagpipes?) providing stirring harmonies while the percussion and the dancers make us feel and see the rhythm. Not all the psalms are quite that loud, of course. Some are about tragedy, guilt, or vengeance. But the songs included within the Bible are strong; they sing about powerful human emotions. Some of these emotions are quite raw (chapter 4 will provide some suggestions for preaching on imprecatory psalms). Again and again, within the book of Psalms and in many of the prophets, we encounter songs that express fiery excitement in loving God.

Is it legitimate for the Bible to present us with songs like these, songs of worship that people sang with great exuberance? Is the Bible on the side of David, leaping and dancing before the Lord? Or on the side of Michal, embarrassed at her husband's energetic dancing in love for the Lord? (See 2 Samuel 6:14-16.) How will you preach on these songs, so that the congregation can feel that same fervor?

Kate broke away from the kiss, scurried into her apartment, and closed the door. Her knees trembled, as she pressed her back against the inside of the door. It was only a kiss, she told herself, don't overreact. But when Warren had stepped close to her, touched her shoulder with his hand, slowly and hesitantly leaned in, she felt her pulse hammering so fast. And as their lips had slowly come together, she was astonished at the feelings that flooded her soul.

It was only a kiss, she told herself again. And yet when you are 28 years old and have not been kissed by a lover since you were seventeen, a kiss is a lot.

She tried to laugh at herself for even thinking the phrase, "kissed by a lover," for although she had been kissed by boys in high school, none of them was ever a lover. And as powerful as that kiss had felt to her, Warren wasn't her lover.

Kate thought she was reasonably good-looking. She had a pretty face and a nice smile and good hair. She kept trim by exercising thirty minutes a week on her StairMaster®, as she watched the late news. Yet, all through college and graduate school she had somehow scared the boys away. She had had lunches with people during her summer internships. The group of her fellow grad students did suppers and movies and parties. But she had not in fact had either a date or a kiss since high school.

So a few weeks ago, her friend, Annette, had set her up with a blind date. It had seemed too corny, too artificial. Kate had refused. But Annette had persisted, and Kate had reluctantly agreed to meet Warren. She had surprised herself, having a pretty good time as they went out to dinner and a movie.

They had gone out four more times, in the succeeding weeks. Kate found herself liking Warren a lot. It was fun to go places with him. He made her laugh.

Earlier tonight, for example. They had gone out to dinner at Chez Marcel. It was quite a bit fancier than the places where they had eaten before. Warren had made reservations for 8 p.m., but when they got to the restaurant, the headwaiter had clucked and checked his reservation book and shaken his head with that ironic half-frown that headwaiters do. (They must teach people how to do this look at headwaiter school; surely they make you practice in front of the mirror until you get it just right, warning you that if you cannot do the ironic half-frown you won't graduate from headwaiter school.) Then the headwaiter at Chez Marcel had said, "I fear we will not be able to seat you for another thirty minutes."

Warren had clucked right back at him, pulled out his appointment book and had shaken his head with the same ironic half-frown, and then he had said, "Fear not, mon ami, for we are not dangerous. We are merely hungry. I see that your book and mine agree that we have a reservation for 8 o'clock, and that's what time it is now. So perhaps you might show us to our table."

The waiter had smiled, showing both good humor and good teeth. Then he had shrugged in that typical French way as he said, "Nothing" (he actually said "nozzing") "Nozzing would give me more pleasure, monsieur. And yet I am afraid I do not presently have a table where I can seat you."

"Again with this being afraid," said Warren, matching the waiter shrug for shrug. "Yet as I said, monsieur, there is 'nozzing' to be afraid of, for it is not peril that faces you. Just two hungry souls, coming in out of the night to dine at your fine establishment."

The conversation had gone on like that for a couple more minutes. Kate hadn't known whether to be embarrassed or to laugh out loud. But there was something about the way Warren presented his comedic responses that soon had her and other customers giggling. And the waiter, too, in spite of his efforts to look stern. After a few more exchanges he had smiled and said he would see what he could do; and had shortly returned to say that the waitress was readying their table, it would take just a moment longer. And when that moment had passed, the headwaiter bowed and began to escort them — followed by a scattering of applause from patrons who had been listening to the byplay — to their table about eight minutes after they had arrived, instead of the predicted half hour.

So Kate had found that it was lots of fun to go out with Warren. But she hadn't felt any strong romantic urges. Actually that thought was pretty amusing all by itself, given her lack of experience, she wasn't sure she would know how to recognize a strong romantic urge.

Until tonight. Until that kiss.

She had never been kissed by a lover. And Warren wasn't her lover.

Yet.

But he could be.

Kate listened for the sound of Warren walking away down the hallway outside her door. She could not hear his footsteps — just the sound of her own breathing, the hum of the refrigerator, the buzz of the clock. Silly, she told herself, the carpet absorbs all the sound, you never hear anyone walking out in the hallway. Of course he is gone, even though you didn't hear him walking away.

But Kate knew, somehow, that Warren had not yet headed out to the parking lot. Somehow she sensed that Warren was still standing, waiting, on the other side of the door, and she had only to let the weight of her hand press down to turn the door handle and she could indeed have a lover, that very night.

Kate stood there, leaning against the door thinking about that, thinking about what it would be like, to be held in Warren's arms. To feel his mouth kissing her again. To be loved by him. Could this be the man she would marry? Her mind flashed to the fairy-tale princess wedding she had dreamed of as a little girl. She had long since given up that idea. Or she thought she had. But could it be, could it be that she would have that wedding, at last, with Warren? Would the two of them make their promises to each other like that? Would he kiss her again, the way he just had, and everyone there would giggle with approval at the rightness of their love? And then — what would their wedding night be like?

Not long ago, I was at a meeting. A friend of mine was in charge. She opened the meeting with prayer. Here is a part of what she prayed. "O Lord, we just thank you, O God, because we are grateful, Father, for all your love, O God, and your mercy, Lord, and we just want to tell you, O God, how much we love you, Father."

This is not a caricature. Those are, as exactly as I can get them, the actual words of the first sentence of her prayer. I have other friends who make fun of prayers like this. The repetition of the address to God, the frequent use of the adverb *just*, they find it funny that anyone would pray this way.

Yet, I think we are likely to miss something, if we laugh too soon. We are likely to miss the realization that this is the prayer of someone who is in love. Deeply, fervently in love. And when you are in love like that, the way you talk isn't about the eloquent articulation of rational coherent sentences — it's about passion. When you are interacting with someone you are passionately in love with, the emotions are intense. When you are angry, you are raging mad. When you are grateful, you are overwhelmed with thankfulness. And when you kiss —

What is it like, to be passionately in love with God? What is it like, when the love you feel for God moves your soul with excitement? Would it be a good thing, preacher, if the people in your congregation felt that depth of longing in their love for God? Would it be a good thing, if your sermons helped them see just how strong their yearning for God really is — and helped them express that love in heartfelt devotion?

Kate did not know if she dared open the door or not. What if she did, what if she and Warren became lovers that very night? She stood their hesitating, shivering. This is ridiculous, she said to herself, I'm not going to stand here like some trembling little fifteen-year-old. She willed herself to walk away from the door. Yet as her feet obeyed, she discovered that her hand had not. Somehow the weight of her hand had pressed down the lever even as she stepped away and the door came open all by itself.

She spun back in astonishment and stared through the open doorway. Warren was no longer there. Kate hardly could say how she felt. Relieved? Disappointed? Upset with herself for opening the door when she had decided not to? Amused at herself for acting more like a trembling fifteen-year-old than she wanted to admit?

Could it be that the love we share with God would be kind of like that?

Could it be that the love of God might move our souls so that we too feel more like a trembling fifteen-year-old than we want to admit?

The children gathered around the old woman in the rocking chair, most of them sitting cross-legged on the braided rug. There were two little ones seated side by side on the old wooden straight-backed chair against the wall. The oldest girl, maybe nine or ten, sat on the little bench, with her little brother on her lap. With hushed intensity, they listened as the old woman spoke.

"Listen to me, children, listen to me. Long years ago, when our ancestors were in slavery in Egypt, the Lord worked many miracles to bring them out of their life of bondage and establish them in a land of blessing. God made a path through the sea for them when they were fleeing for their lives from the army of their enemies, so they could get safe to dry land on the other side. Ah! How amazed they were, so glad to be alive! On through the wilderness they marched, guided by the light of God. Food and water came to them, day by day, given by the hand of the Lord.

"After many days in the desert they came to Mount Sinai. Moses went up on the mountain, and spoke with God. This is when our Lord gave the great covenant, the Ten Words, the Ten Commandments that would guide our people down the generations. You know about the Ten Commandments."

Her frayed Bible had lain open in her lap, though she had not yet read to them from it. Now she held it up and turned it toward the children as she pointed to the Ten Commandments, there in the book of Exodus. The children nodded their heads in response, as she spoke about the Ten Commandments and pointed to them. Some were too young to have learned the Ten Commandments. They had heard them before, but they had not yet memorized them. Some were hearing the story for the very first time. Many of them could not yet read the words for themselves. Even so, all of them nodded. However little they had known before, they knew now, and they nodded.

"Now think on this, my children, think on this. This is the very next thing that happened — the very next thing. No one but Moses was on the mountain itself, when the Law of God was given. All the rest of our people were down at the bottom of the mountain, waiting."

She looked down at the book in her lap, and read:

> *When all the people witnessed the thunder and lightning, the sound of the trumpet and the mountain smoking, they were afraid and trembled and stood at a distance. They said to Moses, "You speak to us, and we will listen. But do not let God speak to us, or we will die."* — Exodus 20:18-19

"They knew our God had worked miracles in the land of Egypt, to persuade Pharaoh to let them go. They knew our God had parted the sea so that they could escape from the soldiers and chariots of their enemies. They knew our God had kept them alive with food and water in the desert. And they were glad that God had done all these good things for them. But now they saw some of the splendor of God's glory on the mountain, and they trembled. They shivered and shook with fear, for they knew that if they got any closer to God, if indeed they were to hear the voice of God speaking to them, they would surely die.

> *Moses said to the people, "Fear not. God has drawn near only to test you, in order that you would fear him, so that you do not sin."* — Exodus 20:20

"Ah, children, children, think on this. Think on the strangeness of what that old Moses said. Such words he said, telling our people they didn't need to be afraid; instead, they just needed to be afraid. He told them God didn't want them to fear; it was simply that God wanted them to fear."

The children pondered on this. It was beyond them, they knew. Sometimes children are fidgety — grown-ups, too. But the children did not fidget. They waited, in the hope that the meaning of this mystery would be revealed to them.

From her rocking chair the woman looked around at the children, one by one. Then she said, "But there was deep meaning in the words of old Moses, my children. The mystery of his words is a little hard to understand, maybe. But you have the wisdom in you, and I believe you can grasp this mystery."

They looked at her, listening with all their hearts. They did not know if they could grasp it or not — but oh, they wanted to — they wanted to.

She said to them, "You know that sometimes you get the shivers. Sometimes because the night wind is too cold, and your blanket is too thin. Sometimes because of a nightmare, and you are so scared. You have all gotten the shivers from these things."

The children nodded once more. Yes, they knew about getting the shivers, from the cold, or from a bad dream.

Then she said, "And sometimes you can get the shivers from one other thing. Sometimes on the way to a parade, or on the morning of your birthday, or on the night before Christmas, a girl or boy will be so excited, excited all the way into the deepest spot in their soul, that they get the shivers. Sometimes, girls and boys just a little older than you fall so much in love, they want to spend the rest of their life together, and when they stand there in the church to say their promises their hearts are so full of love and longing that they get the shivers."

One of the little ones spoke up. "I remember that. I think my sister had the shivers, just like that, when she got married last month."

And the children laughed, and the old woman did, too. Then she nodded as she said, "Yes, Marcy, you're right. I remember that day, too. Chantelle had the shivers. You saw it especially in her because she is your sister, but both of them had the shivers that day, her and Oscar both. Not because they were afraid, and not because they were cold, but because the two of them were so much in love, so excited, so full of gladness."

The children nodded. They remembered that wedding, and they remembered that Chantelle and Oscar had had — something. Something so fine — something called the shivers. They could see it, in that moment. They could see into the mystery of what that old Moses had meant — that God wanted them to have the shivers not from being scared, but from feeling excited and full of gladness because of the way God loved them. So much mystery in the world, so hard to understand, but in this moment the children knew they had grasped at least this much. And it made them glad.

You are well aware, preacher, that words in English can carry more than one meaning; and that words in Greek and in Hebrew are the same way. The way a word carries a meaning is different from how a hiker carries a knapsack, which is different from how a train carries freight, which is different from how an expectant mother carries her baby, which is different from how a new mother carries her baby. The same word, "carries," expresses a range of related meanings. The vivid contrast in the quotation from Exodus points us to the fact that words like "fear" and "afraid" carry more than one meaning. They can mean the deep screaming panic in the face of inevitable approaching death. Or they might indicate only a fairly mild regret. When the headwaiter told Warren, "I fear we will not be able to seat you for another thirty minutes," and "I am afraid I do not presently have a table where I can seat you," he was not expressing terror. His words give us nothing more than a small polite apology — indeed, an apology without much noticeable remorse.

That's a wide range, from mild regret to horrified dread, that can be conveyed in the words, "I am afraid...." So we would be wise not to suppose, when we encounter the term in scripture, that it can only have the meaning of "terror, because pain and destruction are imminent." Clearly that *is* what it means sometimes. Sometimes the biblical writers have chosen the term because they want us to understand that people are scared in the face of danger and death (Genesis 26:7; Jeremiah 30:5; Matthew 14:26; Revelation 18:10; and many more). Much of the time, however, they are pointing us toward the place where our hearts tremble in awe and worship before the glory of God.

> *Were you there, when they crucified my Lord?*
> *Were you there, when they crucified my Lord?*
> *O - o - o - oh! Sometimes it causes me to tremble,*
> *   tremble, tremble.*

Does our religion teach us to live in craven terror, knowing that at any moment the God of all righteousness may decide to sweep wicked sinners like us away to the depths of hell? No. The gospel message is about the love of God, and there is no fear in love, because perfect love casts out all fear (1 John 4:18). God's love for us, then, and the love with which we respond, will not be characterized by fearfulness.

Yet, it also will not be characterized by nonchalance. The scriptures do indeed teach us that the fear of the Lord is the beginning of wisdom (Proverbs 1:7). This fear of the Lord means, first of all, that our attitude toward God will not be an offhand or casual thing, where from time to time we might offer some mild regret for any inconvenience we may have caused, yet without much noticeable remorse.

More than this, fear of the Lord means that our relationship with our Lord will be one where we get the shivers, where we tremble in awe and reverence, in love with Almighty God.

> *Out of the depths I call to you, O Lord.*
> *O my God, hear my cry!*
> *Let your ears be attentive to the sound of my pleading.*
> *If you, O Lord, kept track of our sins:*
> *O God, who could stand?*
> *But there is forgiveness with you,*
> *And therefore....*   — Psalm 130

The text of Psalm 130 notes that instead of keeping a list of our sins, God provides forgiveness. To grasp the power of this assertion more fully, consider the alternative possibility for a moment. Suppose that God did indeed keep track of our sins. Suppose, indeed, that this is the one fact about God that you know most clearly: You know for certain that God has kept careful record of all your sins in specific detail, and therefore you live every day of your life feeling the sick dread of the approaching judgment when God will bring down the gavel to condemn you for those sins. You have, of course, no hope whatsoever that somehow God has failed to record just how consistent your sinfulness has been, and so there is nothing you can do to escape the damnation that shall surely be yours. When the teacher is about to call on you for an assignment you have not done; when your boss is about to catch you in that horrid lie; when your family is about to discover the guilty secret you hoped they would never learn — such humiliations as these can only be a small indicator of the anguish your soul carries day to day. Whenever you consider the consequences of your sin, you shall fall inescapably under the judgment of God, who has kept careful track of every single one of your sins.

Suppose that Psalm 130 had given testimony about this dread by saying something like this:

> *You are the one, O Lord, who keeps track of our sins:*
> *And therefore you are feared.*

If the psalm had said that, the meaning would be clear. God records all of our sins, and we must know that the day will come when we shall receive the just punishment for every single one of them. We live with the crippling anxiety that God's inevitable retribution will be poured out on us.

As it turns out, however, the psalm does not say that. It does not gloss over the danger as if it were not there. We see plainly how terrible the terror could be.

> *If you, O Lord, kept track of our sins:*
> *O God, who could stand?*

But having spoken bluntly of the danger, the psalm sings that our worship does not come from fright, but from the sense of amazement that God should be so generous, so gracious. We do not bow and cringe in God's presence because of our terror of damnation;

rather, we bow in shivering awe and astonishment before the God who offers such forgiveness. We tremble to be so beloved by God.

> *If you, O Lord, kept track of our sins:*
> *O God, who could stand?*
> *But there is forgiveness with you,*
> *And therefore you are feared.*

That's the standard translation. That works, if we remember enough theology, or if you take the time, preacher, to explain this theological point to us when you read us the psalm. Possibly, though, you want to read it to us in a version that gives it to us in such a way that the translation itself carries the psalm's meaning across to those who speak English.

> *If you, O Lord, kept track of our sins:*
> *O God, who could stand?*
> *But there is forgiveness with you,*
> *And that is why we tremble.*

What Kate really wanted to ask, when she and Warren went out to eat the following week, was whether he had indeed remained standing in the hallway for a minute or two, waiting to see if she might open her apartment door and invite him in, the way she had imagined. But she found that she could not ask that question. What if he gave her this puzzled look and said, "No, I walked out to the parking lot, just like always." That would make her look presumptuous and forward. And what if he said, "Yes, I stood there thinking that we might...." If Warren said that, what would Kate say in reply? She didn't know.

So she did not ask — until much later.

As time went on, they discovered many things about their mutual shyness and longing for each other. They learned how to say, "I love you." They found out how to laugh with each other, and how to cry with each other, how to be disappointed, and how to forgive. And it came to pass that they began to discuss wedding details. That's when they discovered how interesting planning a wedding can be.

They had decided on a small, quiet ceremony, with perhaps three dozen invitations sent to family and close friends. This simple plan started to change one evening at the movies. The theatre was showing *The Sound of Music*.[4] Warren had rolled his eyes and laughed when he spotted the ad while he was browsing the movie listings in the paper. Then he had said, "Oh, but why not? Let's do it. Let's go see *The Sound of Music*. Everybody has seen it half a dozen times, and it's corny and all that, but hey, I bet it would be fun. What do you say?" So they had gone and watched *The Sound of Music* together. Kate remembered saying to herself, "Yes, this really is corny." And yet, during some of those tender moments, like when Maria and the Baron were singing to each other out in that moonlit gazebo, as Kate felt her hand enfolded in Warren's, everything about it just felt so right.

And then came the wedding scene.

You remember the wedding scene from *The Sound of Music*. Here comes Julie Andrews, radiant in glory, in her stately processional up the aisle of this great cathedral, surrounded by the affection and support of thousands of guests. All the world has come to share in this celebration. We hear the voices of the nuns singing, and it sounds like angels. What are they singing? Why, it's the same song they sang before, isn't it? Isn't it the song from the beginning of the movie that attempted to reckon with the aggravations caused by the cheery-yet-not-punctual character of the young novice: "How do you solve a problem like Maria?" Ah, but now, *now* this song of exasperation has become a triumphant hymn of glory. Sure, the *words* continue to ask, "How do you solve a problem like Maria?" But the *song* no longer sees Maria as a problem.[5] As we watch the elegant march of the processional, we hear the nuns singing (and maybe it really is angels singing along with them) a song of triumph and goodness, a song that tells us Maria is a child of God, filled with grace.

Kate and Warren sat there holding hands and watching the wedding scene. Somehow, they both realized that this movie wasn't just about Maria and the Baron. The story was about them, about Kate and Warren themselves, about their desire to share their own wedding day with all the world. This is it, they knew, this is what

God had in mind. This is love the way it was always supposed to be.

And so their simple wedding plans grew larger, as they first noticed and then enjoyed and then reveled in the fact that their story was moving toward a moment when they would declare their love, in great trembling gladness, in front of God and everybody.

And thus it came to pass, at their wedding, large and festive and full of joy and grace, surrounded by the love and support of family and friends, and with their own hearts full of the shivers, Kate and Warren offered each other the very best promises they could make. They felt God's blessing touch them, a blessing that made their souls tremble in wonder — and then they kissed. And after the reception, off to their honeymoon they went.

It was on Thursday morning of that honeymoon week, long before sunrise, that Kate awakened her bridegroom with a question. "Warren, do you remember that night we went to Chez Marcel, and you did that hilarious scene with the headwaiter to get him to find us a table instead of leaving us standing there for half an hour?"

Warren chuckled in the dark as he remembered, and nodded.

"And then later that evening, in the hall outside my door, you kissed me for the first time."

"Yes. That was an amazing kiss."

"It made me tremble, and I didn't know what to do, so I ran inside my apartment like a scared little schoolgirl." Kate paused, remembering. And then she said, "So I stood there, pressing my shoulder blades into the back of the door with my heart pounding, and I had just the oddest feeling. It was like I knew you were still standing outside the door; instead of walking out to get your car like usual, I was sure I could feel you standing right outside the door, just inches away from me. And I thought that if I opened the door you would be there, and you would come in and ... well, I wasn't sure what would have happened next. I have always wondered whether that was real, or whether I imagined the whole thing."

"Really," said Warren. "What an interesting notion."

An interesting notion. Is that what the love of God is? Is it just an interesting notion? Or is God's love for us so vibrant that the passion of Jesus would be to come and die to redeem us? What kind of response will this love inspire within us? Consider this well, preacher; how will your sermons from the psalms reflect the passion of God, so that our hearts tremble with joy at God's goodness and majesty?

Exercise 3-2
1. Read through half a dozen or so of the following psalms: Psalm 29, 65-67, 89, 97-98, 145-150. Notice the exuberance and glee within the texts. Read them out loud; read them slowly; let yourself feel the passion in the trembling heart of the singer. What is it about the love and devotion of these writers and singers that makes them sound ardent, rather than prosaic, as they offer their hearts in worship to God?
2. Choose one of these psalms, one where the singer's ardor toward God strikes you in a particularly vibrant way. Write a paragraph or two about that love. What words does the psalmist use to describe it? What actions are visible? Consider why the psalmist might feel so passionate.
3. Create a love story that can show us the eager longing of human love. You'll need a couple who are falling in love, or rediscovering love, or rekindling love. Give them names that touch the right chord for you. Provide some background: How old are they, what do they do, has their relationship just begun or have they endured some hard times together? Possibly you can tell the story from alternating points of view, but usually that's pretty hard, especially within the time limitations of a sermon. Decide from whose perspective the story will unfold. You can tell us a little about their feelings, but mostly you'll just show us, in action and in dialogue, how those feelings get expressed.
4. Weave into your story moments that connect us with the passionate love expressed in the psalm, so that we can feel the ardor of the lovers inviting us to express our own ardor toward God.

"Really," said Warren. "What an interesting notion."

"Oh," said Kate, "so you weren't standing there, outside the door, after all?"

"It was very odd," Warren confessed. "I stood there for a couple minutes, just lost in this shivery kind of daze. I remember reaching out to knock, and then pulling my hand back. Twice. And after that I just shook my head and snickered at my own nervousness as I headed down the hall."

Neither of them spoke for a long moment and then Kate said "I didn't mean to open the door" just as Warren said, "And then I heard a door opening," and they both giggled.

"All I meant to do was go sit quietly at the kitchen table for a minute or two," Kate said, "but it was like my hand had a mind of its own, and as I stepped away from the door, the handle went down and the door opened behind me all by itself. I spun back to the doorway, blushing and clueless about what I was going to say if you were standing there, but you had gone."

"No," said Warren. "I had just turned the corner into the stairwell when I heard an apartment door open. The sound froze me in mid-stride — ready to go downstairs, wanting to turn on my heel and run back. But I couldn't tell if it was your door or someone else's, and I thought about what a fool I'd look like if I went racing down the hall to collide with one of your neighbors coming out into the hall."

"I guess we were both a little scared that night, weren't we?"

"I guess we were," said Warren, and then he kissed her.

"I still tremble when you kiss me," she said, "but not because I am scared."

> *If you, O Lord, kept track of our sins:*
> *O God, who could stand?*
> *But there is forgiveness with you —*
> *such astonishing grace you give us!*
> *— and that is why we tremble.*

---

1. Andrew Greeley, *The Rite of Spring* (New York: Warner Books, 1987). As an aside, Protestants interested in evangelism should read Greeley's *The Cardinal Virtues*, and then ask themselves what it is that makes that story's Catholic parish so appealing, and what lessons Protestant evangelism could glean from that.

2. I wonder though, is it really such good grounds for scoffing? If they felt embarrassed, that only makes them pretty much like the rest of us, in our clumsiness about human sexuality.

3. For a further theological discussion of the Hebrew term *qannah*, passion, see chapter 6.

4. Howard Lindsay, Russel Crouse, Ernest Lehman, and Richard Rogers, *The Sound of Music* (1965); directed by Robert Wise; based on Maria Augusta Trapp, *The Trapp Family Singers* (1949).

5. Consider again the exercises from chapter 1, which show how phrases like "all right" and "Isn't this why you get it wrong?" can express very different meanings, depending on the emotional coloring of your voice when you say them. Notice, then, how at one point in the movie the phrase "How do you solve a problem like Maria?" can express annoyance and frustration, while at a different point it can express respect and glory.

Chapter 4

Hurl Their Babies Against The Rocks

preaching imprecatory psalms as a story

Once upon a time there was a man named Nathaniel. When he was 27 years old, he thought that God must love him very much, for he had about as good a life as a man could want. He had a beautiful wife, Deborah, who loved him. He had five wonderful children, who thought he was the best father in the world. And he had a great job. He was a musician. He sang and played in a small band. He didn't suppose they'd ever be world famous, but people liked their music, and they had a lot of fun.

Sometimes Nathaniel thought about his two older brothers, still running the family farm; feeding the world, and yet, day by day sweating under the hot sun and breathing the dust of the field. He thought about his baby brother, now an expert stonemason, strong as an ox from years of lifting and shaping rock, carving the stone for beautiful buildings, and yet day by day sweating under the hot sun and breathing the dust of the quarry. And Nathaniel thought, being a musician sure beats working for a living.

Nathaniel loved his wife. He loved his children. He loved his work. He loved his friends and his community. He loved his nation. He loved his Lord with deep religious passion. Many of his prayers were songs of praise and devotion, and his heartfelt plea was this: "O God! Let it stay this way forever!"

But it did not stay this way forever. When Nathaniel was 28 years old, the war started. War is never pretty, but this became a particularly bitter war, full of cruelty. Soon there was famine. Many people starved. Yet, somehow Nathaniel and Deborah kept their family alive.

Then, finally, the war was lost.

What happens after the fighting stops is often even worse than the war itself. This conquest was probably about average, in its ugliness. It was the year 587 BC, and the city was Jerusalem. The conquering army of the Babylonians ripped apart the city, to plunder everything and everyone of value. Every man and woman, every child old enough to stand the march to Babylon, would be driven like cattle to a far-off land, where they would be sold as slaves. The conquerors would leave behind only the old women, who would soon starve.

When the soldiers came to Nathaniel's house, they saw his harps hanging on the wall in all their splendor. Nathaniel saw the terrible greed in their eyes, as they lunged to grab them, but a sharp word from their officer stopped them. The officer ordered Nathaniel to wrap the harps in their leather covers. Then the soldiers tied Nathaniel's hands behind him, slung his harps across his back, and dragged him to the street, where he was chained with the other future slaves.

The two older children were tied as well, chained into a line with other preteens from the neighborhood, and marched away. Nathaniel watched them go, feeling the horrible dread that he would never see them again.

Miriam, his beautiful five-year-old daughter — one swipe of a soldier's sword, and she was dead. The soldier laughed. Nathaniel stood there, trembling, helplessly chained among the other slaves, the gorge rising in his throat.

Deborah and the two smallest children had hidden in a corner of the roof. Could it possibly be that they might escape detection? Nathaniel hardly dared to hope. The enemy had now stripped their house bare. Most of the soldiers had moved on to other houses. Then one of the soldiers boosted his comrade to climb to the roof.

Nathaniel saw a horrifying leer come over the soldier's face. It was a look he would later identify as the look of pure evil. The soldier grabbed their baby girl out of Deborah's arms. With one hand he slapped Deborah aside, and with the other he flung the child high in the air, and she fell with a horrifying crunch to the flagstones in the street. Nathaniel shook with rage, straining helplessly against his bonds. He heard Deborah's wails of anguish, and the rude mocking of the soldiers in the street. And then the screams of his son, his little boy Josh, not yet three years old, shrieking "Mommy! Daddy!" as the soldier grabbed him by one arm, swept him around in circle, and hurled him from the roof. He hit the ground at an angle, his leg breaking beneath him, flesh tearing as he skidded across the paving stones. The pain radiating from his son hit Nathaniel like a body blow. He sagged to his knees, unable to breathe, choking on his own despair. Nathaniel watched as little Joshua's life ebbed away, the screams tapering down to desperate little gasps, and finally to one last reedy whimper, "Daddy. Help me." And then — silence.

The soldier on the rooftop had tied Deborah's hands and then tossed her down into the arms of the other soldiers, who caught her — valuable merchandise here — and pawed at her and laughed and made crude jokes. They chained her into a line of women, and marched them away. Nathaniel had roused himself for one brief moment, shouting to Deborah that he loved her, she must be strong and stay alive. Then she was gone. Just as with the two older children, he felt the dread that he would never see her again.

He tried, of course. He tried to get some word about them, during the long forced march to Babylon. The caravan stretched for miles. Nathaniel had no way of telling if he was near the front of the line or close to the back, or where anyone in his family might be. There were a thousand rumors, but no actual information. When they arrived in Babylon, Nathaniel and his harps were quickly sold to a rich landowner who was purchasing musical slaves. Nathaniel never saw or heard any word about his wife and children again.

The history of war is full of stories like this. Tales of harrowing grief that leave their mark deep in the soul of individuals and nations — anguish, hatred, despair. Feelings like these, so severe, can become forever embedded in our souls.

Tell me, preacher, what will the word of God say to us, the members of your congregation, when our hearts rage against our enemies for the things they have done to us?

Enemies? Us?

You don't have to be in the preacher business very long to notice how people shy away from admitting they have enemies.

Christians experience the same feelings of betrayal and hatred and vindictiveness as anyone else. Yet when people do things to us that make us feel that way, we rarely call those people enemies. Our nation may have enemies. People who have suffered greatly from war or devastation might have enemies. But as for the rest of us — we seem to reserve the term "enemy" to mean "someone who hates you enough that they're actively working to kill you, no matter the consequences." And, while we may have some problematic relationships here or there, no one is currently trying to murder us. Thus, few of us will qualify for having any enemies.

Something interesting happens, however, when we insist that only a life-and-death kind of hatred counts. There are all kinds of people who have troubled us, some of them quite severely — those who have betrayed us, people who misled us in order to gain financial advantage, and people who knowingly caused us physical harm. We may feel quite bitter toward them. We might simply not want to have anything further to do with them. We might harbor secret get-even fantasies about them, but it would never come to the point of actual murder. As long as we have never hated them enough to try to kill them, as long as they have never hated us enough to try to kill us, then we can go our whole life and never have an enemy. That might let us avoid the pinch of Christ's command to love our enemies — which is, after all, a very difficult command to contemplate.

Peter copied off Alan's test paper, and then (fearing that the teacher might notice the similarity of answers) accused Alan of cheating from him. As a result, Peter got a high mark on the exam, but Alan got a zero.

Two days before the prom, Mindy sneaked into Jessica's closet and cut several slashes in her dress. When Jessica went to get ready on prom night and found that her dress had been ruined, she was so devastated that she stayed home in tears, and Mindy became the queen of the prom.

When Corinne opened the letter from her landlord, she expected it would be her security deposit refund; instead it said that her deposit would not be returned, because of unspecified damages to the apartment. Corinne was helpless to do much about it, since she had already moved a thousand miles away to start her new job.

Although his teasing sometimes had a sharp edge to it, Andrew didn't think his humor ever really hurt anyone. To Willard, though, it didn't seem like an accident that Andrew kept embarrassing him. Because of this, Willard managed to get a couple of rumors started about Andrew, and in the end, those rumors got Andrew fired.

If we were to ask Alan how he feels about Peter, it would not be surprising if he answered, "I hate him." Presumably Jessica would say something like that about Mindy as well. It's hard to imagine Andrew and Willard being lifelong friends. Will they end up hating each other, instead? And what of Corinne and her landlord?

People will have strong feelings in all these unpleasant circumstances. Yet, most likely, no one in these four scenarios would attempt to murder the person who did them wrong. If that's what it takes to count as an enemy, then perhaps none of these would count as having an enemy. The scriptures instruct us that we must love our enemies.[1] But if we never have any enemies, then this is a command that we will never have to worry about putting into practice.

Jesus once told a story that has become quite famous; it has become known as the parable of the good Samaritan (Luke 10:25-32). He told the story — possibly making it up right on the spot — in the middle of a conversation with a man we would describe as a seminary professor.[2] Within this conversation the professor had just asked a question, and Jesus told the story as a way of answering that question. Jesus and the professor had come to a tacit consensus that "loving your neighbor" is one of the necessary virtues of a godly life. That's when the professor asked his question, "Who is my neighbor?" The motivation behind his question is something like this, "All right, I accept that I must love all those who genuinely count as my neighbors, but if people don't qualify as neighbor, I don't have to love them, I can ignore them or treat them shabbily or however I like."

Is that the same motivation that makes us so reluctant to recognize our enmity against those who have hurt or betrayed us? Our Lord commands us: "Love your enemies." But if certain troubling people don't actually qualify as enemies, we would be free to ignore them or treat them shabbily or however we like.

Michael Dukakis, then governor of Massachusetts, was the Democratic nominee for president in 1988. Among other things, he was an articulate opponent of the death penalty. He also appeared to many to be a cold and emotionless man.

During the nationally televised debate on October 13, 1988, CNN reporter, Bernard Shaw, began with a brief statement of the rules, and then immediately addressed this question to Dukakis: "Governor, if Kitty Dukakis were raped and murdered, would you favor an irrevocable death penalty for the killer?"[3]

Perhaps it is fair to probe presidential candidates this way, with rude personal shock tactics. If you want to be president, you have to be willing to deal with whatever issues and events the world throws at you. Dukakis was not flustered by the question. He responded by depersonalizing it. He declared that he had never thought that the death penalty was effective as a deterrent against violent crime, and he spoke about how other means of deterring crime seemed to be working quite effectively in Massachusetts. Most of his response was given to expressing his hope that larger enforcement and education efforts would win the war against drugs.

The strength of Dukakis' answer was his ability to not take it personally; neither the hypothetical crime nor the abrasive question. It was an excellent demonstration of his style of dealing with stressful situations. Whatever questions might come his way, he would respond by seeking to establish the best, most effective policy.

But the weakness of his "thoughtful policy" reply was that he appeared not to realize how harsh and emotion-laden the question was. Dukakis had not simply been asked about the most effective way to deter violent crime, he had been asked about his feelings. And his response appeared to indicate that he would have no feelings even in the face of a brutal crime against his own wife.

Most preachers have learned to recognize that a lot of questions about facts come with various emotional undercurrents attached. Sometimes people ask you, "Why did God allow this to happen, pastor?" or "What does the Bible say about the death penalty?" or "Should we allow someone who has committed adultery to serve as a deacon?" Any experienced minister comes to know that these are not emotionally neutral requests for information.

When people ask you about such things, your response needs to acknowledge both the request for facts and the feelings of the person asking. Of these two, the feelings are often far more important to the person listening for your answer. When you preach about emotionally charged topics — "Should we support or oppose going to war?" or "Should we support or oppose the state's proposal to build a new prison in our community?" — you need to know that the congregation is made up of people with strong feelings. You will not do a good job communicating your message if you do not reckon with those feelings.

It is impossible to know if Michael Dukakis could have won the 1988 election. He would have done a better job communicating his message, though, if he had offered something like this as his answer: "If any man did that to my wife, I would hate him forever, and my soul would cry out for his destruction. However, we don't want to run the country based on my feelings, no matter how devastatingly powerful those feelings may be. Here in America we believe in the rule of law, not the rule of hatred. We don't want to make policy based on the rage for vengeance I would feel. We want to make policy based on our best understanding of deterrence and effectiveness." From there he could have gone on to talk about his best understanding of how violent crime can be effectively deterred.

Part of your job, preacher, is to recognize that the people sitting before you on Sunday morning have not come to church simply because they want a better understanding of what makes the most effective policy. They have brought a lot of feelings with them as well; some of which will be feelings of betrayal, feelings of hatred, and feelings of bitterness. You can explain to them the Christian virtues of forbearance and forgiveness, and at some level they will probably agree that those are Christian virtues, but this will usually not touch the place in their soul that most needs to hear the Word of God.

The imprecatory psalms (and similar passages in the prophets and elsewhere) enable us to reckon with the hatred and enmity that people really feel. In themselves they do not tell the whole story, but they do indeed tell part of the story, a part of the story that we are not wise to ignore.

As a preacher, you want to cooperate with the ministry of the Spirit, who intends for the children of God to become like our heavenly Father, forgiving those who have become enemies. It will be the work of the Spirit to move us from enmity to forgiveness, but your role as preacher will be part of the means the Spirit uses to accomplish this in people's lives. Your preaching strategy is, therefore, to tell a story where people can see this dynamic in action in someone's life. Let us feel the hatred, strong enough that it touches the hatred in our own heart. Let us feel how hard it is to follow the God of grace. Your hero may well know that it is a good thing we serve the kind of God who is compassionate and forgiving toward all the wicked and foolish sinners, because that is the only hope for any of us. Yet, your hero wants vengeance, and wants God to smite this enemy. It is hard to believe in forgiveness when you are the victim of terrible suffering. Let us feel that struggle as your hero experiences it.

There are four notions that need to show up somewhere within the story, to be fair both to the reality of human experience and to the overall message of the scriptures:

- There are people that I hate, enemies, those who have done me wrong in various ways. Many texts of the Bible give vivid expression to the power of hatred in the human heart.
- My Lord calls me to love my enemies. Jesus intends to redeem my enemies just as much as he intends to redeem me, and he instructs me to pray for my own forgiveness on the basis of how I forgive those who have sinned against me.
- I don't want to have to forgive those who have injured me. I may simply rage against them, longing for God to pay them back as they deserve. Or I might minimize (to myself and others) how mad I am, so that they do not (quite) qualify as enemies. Then I can ignore them or treat them shabbily or however I like.

- The Spirit of God can move my heart, from enmity to forgiveness. It is not easy, but God's kingdom can come, God's will can be done, on earth — and in my heart — as it is in heaven.

These four points will not be the four points of your sermon, of course; nor will they serve as a plot summary for your narrative. Instead, they are pointers to four themes that need to show up, somewhere within the story that you tell.

There are many ways to be trite when talking about hatred and forgiveness. You could give us some sweet sappy ending tacked on as the conclusion of a story of severe betrayal. As Christians, we take it on faith that God will work for good, even in the most horrendous situations. But we do not swiftly arrive at the place where we can see the good that God has wrought from the ashes. We do not swiftly arrive at the place where we can feel that everything is going to be all right. That means that if your story shows us your hero deciding to be Christian about forgiving his enemies, and then having no further trouble with bitterness in his soul, we might not find this story particularly helpful. It may indeed touch us and encourage us much more if your hero has not yet been able to believe in forgiveness, or has not yet had the courage to try to put it into practice, or has tried and failed, at the point that you stop telling us the story.

The Bible, as a whole, is a happily-ever-after book. In the end, all the glory of God shines forth forever in the hearts of the redeemed in all the world. But it doesn't always happen that way with every single story within the Bible. Instead, we can see how particular biblical narrators chose to tell their story. They told the story a certain way, and stopped at a certain place and up to that chosen stopping point, there hadn't been any gladness or restoration. You want to notice this, preacher, because it reflects quite well the situation of most of us in the congregation. The overall context for every story in scripture is this: God makes everything come out right by the very end of the Bible. Still all kinds of ragged edges and heartbreaks show up, within the individual narratives. As Christians, we believe that in the fullness of the kingdom God will restore all things, but all kinds of ragged edges and heartbreaks show up in our lives as well. As far as we've gotten in the story of our own lives up to today, there may not yet have been any gladness or restoration.

We probably won't make it all the way to the celebration in just twenty more minutes either, as we listen to your sermon this coming Sunday.

That suggests that often we will identify our way into the material your sermon presents if the hero of your narrative has not yet discovered how to put forgiveness into practice and is struggling with what that means. That is likely to be the point where we are most ready to listen to the voice of the Spirit of God, prompting us along the road from enmity to forgiveness.

Psalm 137, one of the psalms of the exile, begins as a psalm of deep sorrow, but by the time we get to the end, another strong emotion has come to the fore.

> *(a) By the rivers of Babylon we sat and wept*
> *when we remembered Zion.*
> *We hung our harps in the poplars there,*
> *for our captors asked us for songs.*
> *Our tormentors wanted songs of joy;*
> *they said, "Sing us one of your Zion songs!"*
>
> *(b) How could we sing the songs of the Lord*
> *while in a foreign land?*
> *If I forget you, O Jerusalem,*
> *may my right hand forget its skill.*
> *May my tongue cling to the roof of my mouth*
> *if I do not remember you,*
> *if I do not consider Jerusalem my highest joy.*
>
> *(c) Remember, O Lord, what the Edomites did*
> *on the day Jerusalem fell.*
> *"Tear it down," they cried,*
> *"tear it down to its foundations!"*

(d) Daughter of Babylon, doomed to destruction:
Blessed be those who repay you
for what you have done to us —
when they take your infants
and smash them against the rocks! — Psalm 137

I have not marked the psalm with the usual verse numbers, but with letters to make it clear how the song addresses itself to four different audiences. Beginning with the lines marked (a) above, it is addressed to us musicians who are recollecting how we went on strike, hanging our instruments in the trees, unable to perform the task that our masters demanded of us. At (b) the addressee changes to Jerusalem, the city that represents our homeland and our religion. The song becomes a prayer addressed to God at (c); a prayer that God will smite those Edomites, the nation-next-door that was not neighborly in the face of our trauma. Finally (d) the psalm speaks to Babylon, the nation that defeated ours, the nation whom we now hate with all our hearts.

Many a Christian has been deeply troubled by the last lines of the psalm: "Blessed be those who ... take your infants and smash them against the rocks!" Many a Christian has wondered how the Bible can offer a blessing like that.

Certainly, if this were the only thing the Bible had to say, it would be troubling, indeed. Yet this is hardly a teaching passage, giving us instruction in the ethics of how to treat children. It is a song — a song that was written within a particular context — a song that grew out of some particular set of events.

Several months after Nathaniel had been sold to the rich landowner, his new Babylonian master decided to host a big picnic. It would be an old-fashioned barbecue in that extensive garden area he had built in among the groves of trees down by the riverside. He would invite all his family and friends, it would be a great party, and they would feast on all kinds of good food. And music! The music would be provided by the new Hebrew slaves that he had bought.

The new Hebrew music slaves had proven to be a little reluctant at first. They had not wanted to play or sing. That was no good.

After all, what's the point of buying musical slaves, if they won't make music? The owner chuckled to himself. He'd withheld their food for a few days, and that had brought them around. By the end of the second month, they had learned how to play all the songs in the Babylon Top Forty. They were quite talented — he was glad he'd bought them.

When he looked out his window, on the morning of the picnic, the master saw that it was going to be such a fine day. He smiled. By midafternoon all the preparations were complete. Down by the riverside they had roasted two whole pigs, half a dozen lambs, and a young ox. The aroma of all that barbecue was enough to make you swoon. The rest of the food and wine were carted out across the field to the garden in the grove. People began to arrive. This was one of the moments of nervousness. What if people didn't show up? But they did. All his friends, his business colleagues, his nephews, and all their families. It was a great success. Everyone loved the food. Lots of good conversation. Quite a number of people pulled him aside to compliment him; they were all quite grateful that he had arranged this get together where people could relax and catch up with one another in the midst of everyone's hectic schedules. And everyone enjoyed the music as well, as the new Hebrew music slaves played and sang all the Babylon "top forty" hits.

Then the master had a great idea.

There was a break between two of the songs, and a bit of a lull in the conversation, and the master spoke up. He addressed both his guests and his musicians: "Dear friends," he said, "as you know, I was able to purchase these new musical slaves, part of the spoil from the wonderful victory our army won, in the war in Jerusalem. These slaves have been doing a great job for us this evening, and I'd like us to give them a nice hand." He paused, and the guests dutifully clapped. No point in clapping a lot, of course. Slaves were slaves, it was their job to do whatever their master wanted. Still, they had played well, they probably deserved a little appreciation, so the guests applauded briefly.

Then the master said, "So far they've just been playing our own fine music, but I think it would be great if they would give us a couple of numbers from their own land. So," he said, turning from his guests to face Nathaniel and his fellow musicians, "sing us one of your happy Zion songs, boys!"

The master smiled at them as he said this — a smile that might have been a smile of invitation. But they already knew that it was not. They had seen that smile often enough to know that the smile meant, "You can do what I want willingly, or you can resist for a while and suffer the consequences, but in the end, you will still do what I want."

But Nathaniel did not care. His rage was hanging by a thread. He did not leap down from the bandstand and attack his master. He did not shout curses at him. He almost did both of those, but he knew that all the musicians would be beaten or killed if he did that, not just himself. He turned away and hung his harp on a branch of the tree in back of him, then he turned back to the master, his arms crossed, frown on his face, his body language declaring "on strike!" for all the world to see.

He held that pose for as long as he dared — six or eight seconds, perhaps. Long enough for everyone to see his defiance; long enough for the master to lose face before his guests, yet not quite long enough for the master to take action and kill all the slaves. Just as the master's face began to shift to rage at the insolence of this slave, Nathaniel raised one hand, offered a little bow of obeisance, and said, "Forgive me, my master, there is a song that would be perfect for this glorious occasion of yours, but I have not sung it in several years. Deign to grant me half a moment to remember well the words, so that I may perform my best for your exalted guests."

It was a lie, of course. Nathaniel had never before sung the song he was about to sing, he was making it up in his head in that very moment. There wasn't enough time to work out all the details. He would have to ad lib some of it as he went along. He resumed his posture, arms crossed, frowning, and yet now his body language indicated a man thinking very hard, almost exactly the same as before, to plant the seed of doubt. Had he in fact been defiant before? He looked just the same as he did now, didn't he? And now anyone could see that he was engaged in a fierce effort of memory, so that he could serve his master's will, isn't that right?

Nathaniel took his harp and began to sing. The guests did not understand the words, of course, the words were Hebrew, often similar to Babylonian in sound and form, and yet different and strange. It was a haunting, lovely melody. Only Nathaniel and the other musicians knew what the words meant. One of the other musicians nodded, took up his harp, and added a soft bass line accompaniment. Another filled in a bit of vocal harmony, humming softly. And with no rehearsal, not even a moment for the musicians to confer together about what they would do, Nathaniel sang.

He sang of the irony of this moment, the Babylonians wanting heartbroken Hebrew slaves to sing happy songs of their homeland for the sake of entertainment. He sang of Jerusalem, and all the feelings for his community, his family and friends, his religion — all of this came pouring forth from his soul. The memory came to him of the slave caravan passing through the villages of Edom, on the way to Babylon. The Edomites had not offered neighborly compassion for their neighbors from Jerusalem, now doomed to slavery. They had taunted them, they had hoped that Jerusalem would be torn apart and left as a ruin of sand and rocks in the barren desert. Nathaniel sang of those Edomites with harsh and bitter hatred in his heart, words of destruction on his lips, yet he made his voice sound like a prayer of fervent longing.

Nathaniel looked at the crowd of guests — Babylonian guests. He let his memory take him back to the day when Jerusalem was captured, and he saw once again the crowds of Babylonian soldiers. He let his soul feel it once again — the death of his children. And he sang. He sang his hope that these Babylonians would suffer, that they would suffer like a bereaved parent, that they would suffer as any man would who saw his children smashed down on the pavement, like his children had been. He sang his hope that their children would be killed in just so cruel a manner. That was the hatred in Nathaniel's heart. Those were the words on his lips. Yet somehow he made his voice sound like he was offering a blessing from God Almighty.

Perhaps he would have sung more. Perhaps he intended to sing more, but suddenly he could not breathe. He could not sing another note and so he stopped, and bowed his head.

All the Babylonian guests leaped up and cheered, with great tumultuous waves of applause. No dutiful clapping here, for the song had moved them, moved them deeply, the pathos and vibrancy of the song and its performance was so gripping, even though they did not understand the words. Nathaniel stood there, head bowed, tears on his cheeks. Perhaps this was all he could hope for, this moment of irony as the Babylonians cheered for a song that prayed for their misery.

So the great picnic came to a close. The guests gathered up their things, to make their way home. The cooks and waiters piled dishes into carts, to carry them back to the house and begin the work of cleaning up after such a gala event. The musicians packed up their instruments.

A young Babylonian girl, perhaps five or six years old, broke away from her family for a moment, and ran up to the stage. She had a flower in her hand, plucked from among the reeds down by the river's edge. She came up to Nathaniel, and offered him the flower — a little-girl smile on her face. His hand reached out to take the flower, almost an automatic gesture. Suddenly she was shy, intimidated at addressing this stranger, but she managed to say, "I really liked your song." She placed the flower in his hand, and ran back to her family.

Nathaniel watched her run off. In his soul he tried to sneer, "O daughter of Babylon, I hope you're the one who gets smashed against the rocks, and your parents get to feel the pain I feel!" Yet he felt an unexpected flush of shame as he thought it. He knew well, as all of us do, that it is only if God is compassionate and forgiving toward all the wicked and foolish sinners that there is hope for any of us. His soul raged with hatred, he wanted to destroy them all! Yet he also felt this wrenching ache of grief, this deep longing for his children. Somehow he knew that this grief was not his alone; it was part of the longing of God for all the lost children.

As a student of Old Testament history, you are aware that the historians have put together some fairly substantial data about the siege of Jerusalem and the deportation of its people to Babylon. The Bible gives us a few reports about what happened to the king and to Jeremiah, but we don't have any information about the lives of ordinary citizens. We have no knowledge at all of any incidents from the life of whoever wrote Psalm 137.

Even so, the psalm is there. That means somebody wrote it. That author filled it with intense enmity and despair. Where does such hatred come from? Our best insight into the song's bitter passion will emerge from the recognition that it must have come from some such story as the one I have told.

Is that successful? That's a decision you must make for yourself. Do you understand the psalm better, having heard a story about the rage with which somebody composed it?

If you do, that's a good thing; as I've commented several times, a gain in understanding is always worthwhile. Let me pause for a moment, just to recognize once again that you've picked up that understanding without much *explanation* on my part — what I've mostly been doing in this chapter is *telling a story* I made up about some guy named Nathaniel who sang in a band.

The argument of this whole book is that narrative will often be the strongest way of enabling the congregation to encounter the biblical material. This is especially the case with the imprecatory psalms. It is not hard to create a narrative to present these texts. The technique has two parts. The first part simply is to listen to the psalm, seeking to hear the story behind it: a story of anguish and bereavement, despair and hatred. The commentaries on Psalm 137 will point you (in factual, prose style) to the historical setting: the destruction of Jerusalem, the beginning of the exile. Your job is to hear the stories behind that factual historical prose, stories of the broken lives and broken hearts of all those people marched off to Babylon to become slaves. The second step in the technique, then, is to put that story together in terms of the feelings and experiences of one individual. The exile involved many thousands, not just one person, but I have told it here from the perspective of one man. That makes it feel very personal.

There are two results of following this process. First, by letting us get to the harsh words of the psalm within the context of the story, we understand those harsh words within the psalm more clearly than we would have, from an expository sermon on the meaning of those words. Second, we hear the pain and hatred in someone's heart, and sympathize with it and connect with our own feelings of pain and hatred.

The second of these results is probably the one that's most important, because it's in that second one that we just might be open to the prompting of the Holy Spirit, who wants to move us a little further along the path from enmity to forgiveness.

It is possible to live in bitterness, all the days of your life. As Christians, we believe that it is the will of God for us to love and forgive those who have made themselves our enemies; just as Christ taught us that God the Father has loved and forgiven those who have made themselves his enemies. Yet it is possible, even so, to live with bitterness in your soul against your enemies, all the days of your life.

It is the intention of the Holy Spirit to transform us — to move us from enmity to forgiveness. You can help out in that task, preacher, by telling a story where the Spirit of God might take the opportunity to prompt us to recognize the truth about the hatred within us, and what it would mean to forgive our enemies, and how willing or unwilling we might be to allow God's Spirit to move us further along that path.

Exercise 4-1

Consider again these four scenarios. They each provide a significant amount of plot in just two sentences.

1. Peter copied off Alan's test paper, and then (fearing that the teacher might notice the similarity of answers) accused Alan of cheating from him. As a result, Peter got a high mark on the exam, but Alan got a zero.
2. Two days before the prom, Mindy sneaked into Jessica's closet and cut several slashes in her dress. When Jessica went to get ready on prom night and found that her dress had been ruined, she was so devastated that she stayed home in tears, and Mindy became the queen of the prom.

3. When Corinne opened the letter from her landlord, she expected it would be her security deposit refund; instead it said that her deposit would not be returned, because of unspecified damages to the apartment. Corinne was helpless to do much about it, since she had already moved a thousand miles away to start her new job.
4. Although his teasing sometimes had a sharp edge to it, Andrew didn't think his humor ever really hurt anyone. To Willard, though, it didn't seem like an accident that Andrew kept embarrassing him, so Willard managed to get a couple of rumors started about Andrew, and in the end those rumors got Andrew fired.

Choose one of these, and tell more of the story — perhaps three or four paragraphs. Include some details of time and place (what year? how large a town? were they both church members?). Give us a little of the inner thoughts of the person who has been wronged — how do they feel about this betrayal? The goal is to create enough of a narrative that we can feel the pain and sympathize with the hatred that has arisen in the soul of the person who was wronged.

When I was a sophomore in college I became friends with one of my classmates, a fellow from Queens named Aram. His name was one I had not heard before, so I asked about it. He explained that he was Armenian by background, and that it was a fairly common Armenian name. I really didn't think anything more about that, since everyone in America has some ethnic background or other. Instead, I paid attention to the fact that Aram was uncommonly studious for a sophomore (which gave me access to much better note-taking than my own). He was also a great fan of the New York Mets during the years when the Mets provided very little reason for anyone to believe in them.

Aram and I would sometimes have lunch together after class. Sometimes just for the sake of friendship, but often it was so that I could scan through the notes he had taken during one of the lectures I had missed.

We were sitting at the lunch table one day when some news came on the radio. The announcer mentioned some incident in the nation of Turkey. I don't recall what it was. I was not paying much attention. Then that changed. I was paying complete attention, but to Aram rather than to the radio. It was a stunning transformation. Aram was talking about the Turks, the terrible things that the Turks had done, the Turks had come in the night, they had attacked, we had done nothing to deserve this, but the Turks came and destroyed our town. The Turks had killed the children, the Turks had come and killed all our children.

I listened in utter astonishment. We were just a couple of nineteen-year-old sophomores — what was all this? Where was my friend, the baseball fan, the straight-A college boy? The rage he felt was intense, so personal that it took me several minutes to realize that the story Aram was telling was not about himself personally. He was speaking of the village where his great-grandparents had lived, in Armenia — yet this experience was so ingrained in his sense of family that he constantly said "we" and "us" as he recounted how "we" were devastated, of how the Turks abused and slaughtered "our" children, of the horrible suffering that happened to "us" — yet all of these events had taken place fifty years before Aram was born.

The transformation was unmistakable. The schoolboy was gone. Sitting across from me in the lunchroom was a soldier, grim and determined; place a rifle in his hands, and he was ready to fight and kill the Turks.

There were two things I thought of to say in response to this. I could not figure out how to say both of them. In the end, I did not succeed in saying either one.

The first thing I wanted to say was something like this: "Oh, Aram. I am so very sorry for the suffering that your family experienced. I know there is nothing I can do to make it so that it didn't happen that way. But I want you to know that I care." I could have said that. I wish I had.

The second thing I wanted to say was something like this: "Aram, how many Turkish children should we murder today, to even things out?"

Hatred and enmity can continue for a lifetime, or even from generation to generation. Even as a nineteen-year-old I could understand how Aram's family had good reason for hating their enemies. Yet I could also see that there was no way for us to go back and change the history so those terrible events never happened and that there was no way that hating Turkish children today could restore the Armenian children of many years ago.

But as a college sophomore I did not have the wisdom to see how to articulate these things. In the end, I said nothing at all. I did my best to listen. I hope I listened well.

Sometimes listening is all you know how to do.

Yet we hope for more — especially from our preachers. We do not want you to stand in the pulpit on Sunday morning and listen for twenty minutes; we want you to preach us a sermon where we can hear God speaking to the most needy places in our souls. Hatred and forgiveness is one of those places. Is there a word from the Lord that will speak to us, is there a way that the grace of the spirit of holiness can transform us, in the places in our souls where we hate our enemies?

Exercise 4-2

Read all the passages in each of these two sections (don't skip this — read these passages!).

1. Nahum 3:1-19; Obadiah 1-15; Psalm 35:4-9; Psalm 94:22-23; Psalm 75:7-8; Psalm 3:7; Psalm 5:4-10; Luke 1:51-53; Revelation 6:9-10.
2. Psalm 96:1-3; Psalm 117:1-2; Isaiah 49:5-6; Matthew 5:23-24; Matthew 5:43-45; Matthew 6:12-15; Matthew 18:21-35; Mark 11:25; Luke 6:27-36; Ephesians 4:32; Colossians 3:12-13.

Notice that the passages in the first part are pretty clear on the destruction of those wicked enemies, yet the second list of passages is about the hope for the redemption of all the world, including our enemies. Give yourself a few moments to ponder on this strong contrast.

The teacher of the fifth-and-sixth-grade class has asked you if you would take a five-minute break from the Sunday school class you usually teach and drop in on her class. She would like you to give a five-minute explanation to her students about vengeance and forgiveness. You've excused yourself from your own class, leaving one of the elders to lead the discussion on the next question, and have hustled down the hall and stepped into the classroom with these youngsters. Give your five-minute lesson to them now.

How are Christians to deal with the level of contradiction we encounter between these two sets of texts? It is worth our while to take a few honest moments to recognize this contradiction. Here are passages that call for the destruction of our enemies, and here are passages that call for the forgiveness of our enemies. We will not be well served by glossing over this strong contrast.

At the same time we might note that this contradiction is just as present within the hearts of the faithful. In vivid language, these texts of scripture reflect the contradiction that is inside us. Anyone who is willing to pay attention recognizes that both of these are true. We do understand the Christian virtue of forgiving those who have wronged us, and in our own hearts we do long for vengeance. Part of your work, preacher, is to touch our hearts in this place where we struggle. You can do that by letting us come alongside someone within the narrative of your sermon who is struggling with enmity in their own soul.

Exercise 4-3

Look again at the scenarios in Exercise 4-1 and the biblical texts in Exercise 4-2. Choose a passage from each section of Exercise 4-2 — one from the vengeance texts, and one from the forgiveness texts and give them to one of the characters who has been wronged. You might give them the text in any of a variety of ways.

1. They happened to pick up Grandmother's old well-worn King James Bible. They opened to where Grandmother had left her bookmark — one of the passages that calls out for destruction of one's enemies. They first read the words Grandmother wrote in the margin, "I know I'm supposed to forgive Helen, but this passage says how I really feel. Smite her, O Lord!" Then they read the passage, and think, "Yes, Lord, that's how I feel, too."
2. In their daily devotional Bible reading, they have come to this passage, one that they have usually skipped before, but this time the desire for destruction of their enemy resonates very clearly. Then at the close of their devotions they pray the Lord's Prayer and get stuck on that "forgive us our debts as we forgive our debtors" line.
3. At the big family dinner last Sunday, their sister asked her son what he had learned in Sunday school that morning. This nephew is in the fifth- and-sixth-grade Sunday school class, quite a bright young lad, and he answered that the preacher had come to their class and showed them the contrast between one Bible verse that talked about vengeance and another that talked about forgiveness. As they overhear their nephew explaining this to his mother, they find that they hear the same contradiction in their own souls.

Write three or four paragraphs in which your hero considers the contrast between the two texts, and struggles with the application — perhaps in conversation with a friend, perhaps in prayer, perhaps in trying to write a letter to their enemy. Move the story along, not to a conclusion but to where we can connect in with how terribly hard it is to forgive people who have done us wrong.

Remember the four pointers mentioned earlier — not as a plot summary, but as items that need to be present somewhere in your story, to be fair to the reality of human experience, and God's gracious call revealed in scripture.

- There are people that I hate, enemies, those who have done me wrong in various ways. Many texts of the Bible give vivid expression to the power of hatred in the human heart.

- My Lord calls me to love my enemies. Jesus intends to redeem my enemies just as much as he intends to redeem me, and he instructs me to pray for my own forgiveness on the basis of how I forgive those who have sinned against me.
- I don't want to have to forgive those who have injured me. I may simply rage against them, longing for God to pay them back as they deserve. Or I might minimize (to myself and others) how mad I am, so that they do not (quite) qualify as enemies, then I can ignore them or treat them shabbily or however I like.
- The Spirit of God can move my heart, from enmity to forgiveness. It is not easy, but God's kingdom can come, God's will can be done, on earth — and in my heart — as it is in heaven.

---

1. Jesus said this in Matthew 5:44 (paralleled in Luke 6:27-28), and demonstrated it in Luke 23:34; as did Stephen in Acts 7:60. Note Paul as well in Romans 12:14 and 1 Corinthians 4:12-13, and also 1 Peter 2:23.

2. νομικος, a teacher of the Law, someone who gives instruction in the five books of Moses.

3. A transcript of the debate can be found at http://www.debates.org/pages/trans88b.html.

Chapter 5

To Make A Long Story Short[1]

preaching multi-chapter texts as a story

In the year 587 BC, the Babylonian army captured the city of Jerusalem. The conquering soldiers tore down the buildings, stole everything worth stealing, and dragged off every reasonably healthy man, woman, and child to become slaves in Babylon. And so began the period of great sorrow in the history of our people — the time known as the exile, or the Babylonian captivity.

Among those taken as slaves were three young men. Their names were Hananiah, Mishael, and Azariah. Their new Babylonian masters told them that they would have to get used to the Babylonian way of doing things from now on. They would have to learn to walk and talk and think Babylonian. They even gave them Babylonian names.

Now Nebuchadnezzar, the king of Babylon, liked being king. He liked the power it gave him. He liked the deference everyone paid to him. He liked the fringe benefits. He liked it all. Yet even though he had it all and liked it all, he still was not satisfied. He wanted more. He decided to become a god.

Perhaps you have discovered, if you've ever tried to become a king, that it is not such an easy thing to do. It helps if you get yourself born to the right parents. It helps to be in the right place at the right time. Even then, it often turns out to be pretty iffy. You might well imagine that becoming a god would be even more challenging.

Nebuchadnezzar recognized that it would take some planning. His plan to become a god went like this: He had an image constructed, sixty cubits high. That's about as tall as an eight- or nine-story building. He had it built in the open fields, just outside the city limits. You could see it for miles.

Then he called in every government official to a special meeting, and this is what he told them. "From now on, everyone has to worship my image. Anytime anyone plays any music, on the bagpipes, on the harp, or any other musical instrument, everybody who hears it has to fall down and worship my image. I want every herald in the land to proclaim this notice." And because Nebuchadnezzar recognized that people might be a little reluctant to accept this right away, he also told them one more thing: "Anybody who doesn't fall down and worship my image will be burned alive in a furnace."

It seemed to work pretty well. The heralds went out and proclaimed. The music played. Everybody in the land fell down and worshiped. Well, almost everybody. Hananiah, Mishael, and Azariah did not. They knew that the God of heaven had created the earth and everything and everyone in it. And they knew that no image fashioned by human hands was going to replace the God who had fashioned those humans. No king, no matter how arrogant, could claim the place of Yahweh. Not in fact, and not in their hearts.

King Nebuchadnezzar felt quite upset by their refusal. His attitude seems pretty harsh. If a person got stuck being the ruler of the biggest empire on the face of the earth, one of the very few negative features would be this: You wouldn't have much opportunity for advancement. Most of us would not feel too troubled about that. But suppose you decided that even though you were already right at the top, you still wanted a promotion. Suppose you decided you wanted to move up, from being a king to being a god. And suppose you had got nearly everyone in the empire to agree that you had, indeed, been promoted to become a god. Tell the truth now, wouldn't you feel pretty well satisfied with yourself? Why would you even bother to notice a few conscientious objectors here or there?

But Nebuchadnezzar was not satisfied. Three exceptions were three exceptions too many. He had Hananiah, Mishael, and Azariah arrested. "Weren't you guys listening?" he said to them, when they were dragged into his presence. "Do you think I was just kidding about this furnace? You guys will do what I say or you're charcoal.

You'd better decide to worship me, because there isn't any other god that's going to rescue you."

Their reply is quite instructive. It is one of those Bible verses that everyone ought to memorize, because the time will come when we will need to know it. What did Hananiah, Mishael, and Azariah say in the face of King Nebuchadnezzar's threat? "We do not know," they said, "whether our God will rescue us or not. But whether he does or whether he doesn't, we will not worship your image" (Daniel 3:16-18).

It's the kind of line you'd expect to hear at the movies — defiance in the face of danger. The difference is that when we go to the movies, we know that the heroes aren't really running much risk. Harrison Ford may get beaten up, and he may have to face impossible situations, but we know that he always wins in the end. We know the movie is not going to end with the hero dying as the villain laughs. By the end of the movie, the good guys are going to triumph despite all odds. We know that, therefore, we don't worry too much about them.

But in real life, the dangers are dangerous, and far more worrisome. In real life, people get hit by cars and they die. People get cancer and they die. People work as hard as they know how to work, and they still lose their jobs. And their homes. And their self-respect. And their hope.

"We believe," said Hananiah, Mishael, and Azariah, "that our God has the power to work miracles. We believe that our God has the power to rescue us from your hand, King Nebuchadnezzar. But we do not know if he will. We do not know if we will live or die. We do not know. But we still are going to worship him, instead of you."

About six centuries after these events would have taken place — which is to say, in about AD 55 — the apostle Paul left the city of Corinth, where he had been doing his missionary work, to return to the city of Jerusalem. There had been some crop failures in Judea and the surrounding countryside, so the local people didn't have much food, or much money to buy food from folks in the caravan and shipping business. The people in the churches of Greece and Macedonia had given so generously, to help the people of Judea buy groceries; and Paul was going to deliver that gift to feed the hungry children of Jerusalem.

You must understand how much he loved those people. They were his countrymen, his cousins, his nieces and nephews, his high school buddies, and his college classmates. Some of them believed, as he believed, that all the hopes of his nation, down the long reaches of the centuries, had been fulfilled in the Messiah Jesus. Others scoffed. Indeed, many of them burned with a great hatred for the followers of Jesus, and for Paul in particular, for he had once been a scoffer along with them.

He loved these people who hated him. As he got ready to leave Corinth to go back to Jerusalem, he wrote his letter to the Christian community in Rome, and in it he revealed some strong feelings. "I am speaking the truth in Christ," he told them. "I am not lying. My conscience bears me witness in the Holy Spirit, that I have great sorrow and unceasing anguish in my heart. For I could wish that I myself were accursed and cut off from Christ for the sake of my brethren, my kinsmen" (Romans 9:1-3).

What might a person do, for the sake of someone you love? What risk might you run? "I would give my right arm," you can sometimes hear a person say. Perhaps, to try to rescue someone you love, you might even dare to run into a burning building. "I would do anything," Paul suggests. "Whatever it would take. Even if it cost me my life, even if it meant that I, myself, would end up cut off from Christ, I would do it."

So Paul and his companions left Corinth, the book of Acts tells us. They traveled north up to Philippi, and then sailed east across the Aegean Sea to western Turkey, and then south through all those Greek islands until they found a ship headed for Syria. They bought their tickets and voyaged to the port city of Tyre. There was a community of Christians in Tyre. Paul and his friends stayed with them for a week. Those Christians discerned, in the wisdom the Spirit had given them, that Paul would be in danger if he went on to Jerusalem. They warned him not to go.

But he was determined to go.

The travelers got back on the ship, and continued their voyage south to the port of Caesarea. That's only about fifty miles from

Jerusalem. While they were staying there, at the house of Philip the evangelist, a prophet named Agabus came down from Judea. Moved by the vision he had seen, Agabus had journeyed those fifty miles, desperate to make good speed on the road so he would get to Caesarea before it was too late, and yet having to check each caravan and each traveler going the other way in case Paul might have already left for Jerusalem. I suspect Agabus did not give himself an hour to check into his room at the Caesarea Shores Holiday Hotel, to take a quick shower and change into his clean suit. Instead, he marched right into Philip's house. Travel grime streaking his face, he marched right into the room where everyone was having church. He marched right up to Paul, right in the middle of the sermon probably, and looked him right in the eye. Then Agabus reached down and unwrapped Paul's belt sash, and he tied up his own hands and feet with it. He said, "The Holy Spirit has told me that this is what they're going to do to you when you get to Jerusalem."

Sometimes when a prophet speaks forth a prophecy, it's hard to understand what it means. But not this time. No one felt uncertain about what this prophecy meant. After the work and sweat of the journey down from Judea, pressing along mile after mile to get to Caesarea in time to issue his warning — after all that, Agabus did not offer up a hesitant or ambiguous prophecy that people might interpret four or five different ways.

The message was clear. It was clear to Paul's companions. It was clear to the church in Caesarea. Everyone begged Paul not to go to Jerusalem.

The message, however, had already been clear to Paul. It had been clear to him before Agabus arrived. It had been clear to him as he considered all the warnings his friends had offered during the journey. It had been clear to him back when he was in Corinth, writing his letter to the Romans, as he set down his heart's sorrow and anguish over his kinfolk back in Jerusalem, as he set down his resolve that he would run any risk — life, death, suffering, even being cut off from Christ if that would do it — anything.

Paul dared to believe that maybe, just maybe, if their friend and kinsman Saul of Tarsus came to the people of Jerusalem just once more with this message of the gospel — and if he came to them with the gift in his hand from the Gentile Christians of Greece and Macedonia, with this tangible demonstration of how the love of God had transformed the lives of those people, so that they gave generously to sustain the lives of people they had never even met — then maybe, just maybe, the people of Jerusalem would listen this time. Maybe, just maybe, they would see that the gospel is real, when they saw the difference this gospel made in the lives of strangers from far away — when they saw how the love of Christ had moved those Greeks to love the people of Jerusalem, and to put that love into practice by giving their money to buy them food when they had no food.

Paul told his friends, "I am ready not only to be imprisoned but even to die at Jerusalem for the name of the Lord Jesus." And they could not persuade him that the danger was too great; for he had resolved that he would make this effort no matter the risk. And so they said, "May the will of the Lord be done" (Acts 21:7-14).

We do not know, said Hananiah, Mishael, and Azariah, if God will rescue us from the burning fiery furnace. We do not know if we will live or die, but we will follow our God and do what is right, no matter the cost. Paul might have said the same thing: I do not know if God will rescue me from imprisonment and death when I get to Jerusalem. I do not know if I will live or die, but I will follow my God and do what is right, no matter the cost.

As all preachers come to know, there are certain passages that resist sermonizing. Sometimes it is because the ideas in them are so complex. You can try your best, but in your allotted twenty minutes you will not be able to explain all the things that need explaining in this text. In other passages, the ideas are not that complicated, but there is still so much material that it's not obvious how to present it fairly within a sermon. It's not that it's too hard — it's just too long. You can select for the morning's reading a brief excerpt from within the overall passage, and then try to provide the necessary context within the sermon itself. That's often the best way to proceed, but it's still quite a challenge.

It is, for example, quite difficult to understand the point of any single passage within the book of Job, apart from an understanding of the entire book of Job. Job's story is a powerful one, offering a great depth of encouragement to those who find themselves in the midst of life's most painful situations, and also to those who hunger to know God more fully. Job remains one of the least-understood and therefore least-read books in the canon. Isn't that a loss that ministers should care about? Well, preacher, what do you have in mind to do about that? You could (just possibly) stand in the pulpit and read the 42 chapters of Job out loud for this Sunday's scripture text — but please don't. If you did, you would end up using the entire time allotted for worship. There would be no time left for you to explain it, draw it together, make it accessible to the congregation, and enable them to find strength from it. Yet you need to find a way to preach the whole book before you preach the excerpts.

It is somewhat easier to consider an excerpt from the Jacob texts in Genesis, or from the passages concerning the exile, although the challenge remains much the same. The overall meaning of Jacob, and the overall meaning of the exile, can only be had by considering the full sweep of the story. But these stories are not to be found in one short passage; they are told across many chapters of the Bible. Consider the loss if we do not know the sweep of these stories. How can we understand what it is to be Israel, if we do not know Jacob? How can we understand the mark the exile placed upon the children of Israel, if the anguish of the exile, and the astonishment of the return, are not part of our sense of heritage? A preacher can certainly preach about prayer and use the example of Jacob wrestling with God (Genesis 32:22-32), even in the awareness that most people in the congregation do not know very much about the Jacob story. We who listen may well glean some helpful insights about prayer from that sermon. Yet it's hard to suppose this will be as rich an encounter as we might have, if we come to the story ready to appreciate the irony of Jacob the heel-grabber, unable to overcome God, unwilling to let go.

Similarly, a preacher can preach about sorrow or hope or rebuilding from texts in Ezekiel or Nehemiah, or from Psalm 126 or 137, in the awareness that most people in the congregation do not know the story of the exile at all. People will encounter the presence of God in those sermons, even without that background. Surely we should feel a lament for how members of the congregation end up settling for just a fragment of what they might discover, if they understood how these texts tremble with the devastation in the souls of generations of God's people.

What's a preacher to do? Sometimes it feels like we can only shrug. If people are going to grasp these passages, it will have to happen because of their own reading, in their personal devotions, and in their small group Bible studies. If they themselves would read the Bible, regularly and gladly, they would begin to see these extensive multi-chapter connections as an ongoing part of their own religious life. But Sunday sermons cannot make that happen for them. It would be nice to be able to explain all this biblical material to the congregation, providing the background that they need to see the big picture, but there just isn't time. As a preacher, you decide to stick to passages where eight or ten verses form a cohesive unit; then you preach from your selected text, for your allotted time.

Even so, it is possible to step beyond that feeling of wistfulness.

For starters, you could incorporate two small incremental steps in your preaching. First, when you are preaching from a passage of ten verses, such as the Valley of the Dry Bones (Ezekiel 37:1-14), you could take a brief moment — no more than two minutes — to recount for us a *Cliff Notes* summary of the exile; that will mean we will remember it a little bit better next time you make a reference to it. Second, when you are encouraging daily Bible reading from the pulpit, you can suggest that many members of the congregation are now ready to move beyond prepackaged magazine devotionals to *lectio continua*,[2] so that we can begin to discover themes and plotlines that extend across many chapter divisions.

Beyond this, every once in a while you really can offer a sermon that covers multiple chapters of the Bible. It is possible to do this with integrity, within your allotted time. One clear way to make this happen is to discern a particular narrative line that weaves through the material, and then to tell that story.

Take, for example, the material in Romans chapters 9 through 11. It is two or three pages of fairly dense reading with some rather obscure allusions,[3] as Paul considers the place of Israel in God's plan, now that Jesus has come. It is certainly possible to skip over this material. Some Bible study booklets on Romans do exactly that. You can read through the end of chapter 8, "Nothing in all creation will be able to separate us from the love of God in Christ Jesus our Lord!" And then you can pick up with Romans 12:1, "I appeal to you therefore, by God's mercies, to present yourself as a living sacrifice, holy and acceptable to God; this is your spiritual worship." The sureness of the grip of God's love in chapter 8 can readily be the motivation for the exhortations in chapter 12.

Yet the material we would skip over that way offers us three chapters on the topic of the place of Israel in God's plan, now that Jesus has come. Most Christians find that to be a subject of more than passing interest. In our pluralistic age, it also applies readily to the question of the place of other religions in God's plan. Moreover, these chapters offer some probing insights into topics like faith, evangelism, and salvation. We could avoid this material, because we reckon it will be too lengthy if we present it cohesively and too shallow if we present it atomistically. But if we do, we will miss out on a lot.

The key to enabling a congregation to get hold of these three chapters (or to get hold of any unit greater than twenty verses or so) is to ask, "Can I discern a narrative line within this material?" Sometimes more than one narrative line may suggest itself to us but we only need one. Perhaps we can recognize such a possibility in Paul's words from Romans 10:1, "My heart's desire and prayer to God for Israel is that they might be saved." That is, there is a narrative line available concerning how Paul longs for the salvation of his people. So in preaching the material within these three chapters, we could tell that story: The story of Paul's determination to find a way to bring the gospel to his cousins in Jerusalem, even though many of those cousins were out to get him.

There are a number of ways to go about that. Earlier in this chapter, I offered a simple journey model, with Paul on his way from Corinth, stopping in Caesarea in his way to Jerusalem (with the exile story of Hananiah, Mishael, and Azariah hovering in the background, as a way of highlighting the anxiety inherent in not knowing what God might do). But there are plenty of other ways to get hold of that narrative line.

Exercise 5-1

Take eight or ten minutes to try out one of the following three scenarios. Read through all three of them, and pick the one you like. Read that paragraph once or twice more. Then close the book, and go ahead and begin telling the story out loud, in your own words, making up the rest of the story's details as you go along. (Yes, I know that some of you are still resisting that "do the exercise out loud" instruction. And you may indeed feel intimidated at the thought of getting stuck in mid-phrase somewhere in your storyline, along with the sense that that will feel even more awkward if you are saying your words aloud. It could happen that way, of course. It nevertheless remains true that you will profit more from the exercise if you speak audible words. Even if your words sound clumsy, you will hear the story better now, and preach it better later on. Be brave, preacher, and do the exercise out loud.)

1. Consider this story from the perspective of one of the named-but-still-pretty-obscure characters from one of those Greek or Macedonian churches — Stephanas, perhaps, or Epaphroditus. What would it be like to find yourself musing once again about how this fellow Paul came to your community, preached the gospel about Jesus, and people came to believe it? Then the word came about the famine in Jerusalem, and in great generosity the people in your church decided to gather up a large sum of money to provide food for those people far away. You remember how moved Paul was by this. You remember as well how it set a great hope in his heart; that if he himself were to deliver this financial gift, this could be the moment when those who had rejected the gospel would themselves be astonished, and want to know what it was that had moved the heathen to offer such financial sacrifice on behalf of God's people. Now Paul and the gift are on their way, they sailed

off several weeks ago, and all you can do is pray, not knowing how it might be turning out, in far-off Jerusalem.

2. What would you be thinking if you were one of Paul's companions during this journey — Luke or Timothy, or maybe Aristarchus — as the group draws steadily nearer to Jerusalem? Perhaps you would feel the sick dread of how badly it could end. You find that Paul almost agrees with you. He acknowledges that the project could easily result in his death. Nevertheless, he continues full of hope. He is not afraid of dying, and he even reckons that his willingness to deliver the gift in spite of the risk — or the reality — of losing his life, will be part of the testimony of what the love of Jesus moves us to do. All right, you understand that possibility, too. You pray that it will come true, before Paul pays that price. But most of all, you are afraid.

3. Perhaps Paul, the famous writer of letters to churches, also dropped a line to his old college roommate, Baruch, still living back there in Jerusalem. At one time, Baruch and Saul were the very closest of friends, but now Baruch burns with the anguish of shame and betrayal because Saul had pledged his allegiance to this Jesus. He remembers when Saul had come to visit him and his family a few years back. Dinner had gone pretty well, but after dinner Saul started talking about Jesus, and Baruch had become infuriated and insisted that Saul leave. The memories are pretty bad. The nightmares are worse. The rage in Baruch's soul comes out in this recurring dream, where he has to be the one to cast the first stone at the execution of his friend Saul for blasphemy. What would that feel like, if you were Baruch, waking up in a sweat, your pulse hammering? And that's not the only nightmare. There's another one, because you and your family are among those struggling with not quite enough to eat, in the food shortage that is gripping Jerusalem. You feel the great dread of the day when you will have nothing to feed your children. So it was an astonishing thing, to read in Saul's recent note that

he is bringing a gift from the churches of Greece to help feed the people of Jerusalem — to help feed your family. After the things you said to Saul, you cannot fathom why he would ever want to see you again, let alone why he would want to offer a gift in such compassion. And you can see no way to resolve this puzzle.

Simply by doing that much of an exercise — selecting and filling in the details for the friend praying from afar model, the traveling companion model, or the letter to the roommate model — you will find yourself better than halfway to a very preachable sermon. You now have a strong and moving narrative framework. To complete the job, you can easily select a handful of excerpts from the three chapters in Romans, and interweave them into the story line, as Paul's conversational voice within the narrative. That is, let Stephanas muse on the kinds of things Paul was saying, before he headed for Jerusalem (perhaps it was the conviction that in God's view there is no distinction between Jew and Greek, and therefore everyone who calls on the name of the Lord will be saved). Or let us overhear Aristarchus and Paul in conversation, watching the sunset from the deck of the ship. Perhaps Aristarchus is feeling a little proud that he now holds a place with God that Jews no longer do, and Paul uses his olive tree metaphor to admonish him to reverence, awe, and humility. Or, let Baruch struggle with the fact that even though he intended to forget about Saul after he threw him out of his house, some of the things Saul said to him keep coming back to his mind, especially the one about how the gifts and calling of God are irrevocable.

When you have done that, you have created a sermon that your congregation will find both memorable and helpful. It will give them a good basic overview of the material in Romans 9-11. And they will feel like they understand the point of those chapters, perhaps for the very first time.

You could argue, of course, that they will have at best a very light understanding of the material found there, and that paragraph after paragraph cries out for deeper explication. What about texts like "Why then does God find fault? For who can resist his will?" and "all Israel will be saved" and "God has imprisoned all in disobedience that he may be merciful to all" — don't these passages need more than a brief mention, if people are going to understand the depth and complexity of Paul's argument? Of course that's right. Still, isn't it also right that people need to start somewhere when they have never read this material (let alone studied it), and that a beginner's minimal grasp on what Paul is saying here is just such a start? That is: Wouldn't an overview of where Paul is going, a sense of the big picture, be a solid first step in understanding the details that make up that big picture?

All right. Suppose you feel like you want to explore the details of these three chapters with your congregation, more than you feel you could with any of the three narrative patterns I've suggested. What then? Here's another possibility.

What if you were to offer your congregation a sermon on a difficult topic, using brief citations and allusions to a dozen different books of the Bible, expecting them to get the references and put it all together in their own minds? That's essentially what Paul did, in Romans 9-11. It's hard to imagine there could be very many congregations in which that would work. Across the vast majority of churches, if you attempted to offer such an array of material, drawing from twelve different books of the Bible, surely most people would find themselves unable to keep up with the page turning, let alone the overall argument. Yet when Paul wrote to the congregation in Rome, he apparently anticipated that some of the people there would indeed catch his allusions and get his point. Rome was a place he had never visited, but he knew quite a number of the church leaders there, from occasions where his travels and theirs had overlapped. Thus it seems he was confident that there were people in the church in Rome who would know their Bibles well enough to understand his references and follow the argument he made in these three chapters.

Even so, there would have been plenty of people in the church in Rome who would not have anywhere near the background they needed to do that. Some of them were children, who were still just learning the names of the books of the Bible. Some of them were new converts, who had never read the Bible before. Others were people who felt embarrassed about their lack of Bible knowledge; people who kept saying they wished they knew the Bible better, but never quite seemed to get around to doing anything about that.

Exercise 5-2

What would it be like, to be one of the members of that congregation in Rome, hearing Paul's letter read during a Sunday church service? Perhaps you are one of the children, perhaps one of the newer members, or perhaps one of those embarrassed people who have kept meaning to develop a Bible reading habit, but haven't succeeded yet in making that happen. You are trying to keep up, but you're not doing too well at it. You hear quotations from books of the Bible you've never heard of. You see that the lines the preacher is reading seem to mean a lot to the people in the next row, but honestly you haven't a clue what those lines are about. The preacher seems so enthusiastic, like this is wondrous and vital information, but the message is as clear as granite to you and honestly the whole deal just feels frustrating.

Now, as a twenty-first century preacher, select one major point from these three chapters, the one exegetical crux you want your present congregation to grasp. Consider how the other material in Romans 9-11 helps strengthen that understanding. Then try out one of these:

1. Tell the story of sitting in church, in first-century Rome, from the perspective of an almost-teenager of eleven or twelve. Your parents have become quite active in the church community, but you're not really sure if you want to be part of this or not. You are not as surly this morning as you sometimes are; but once again you mostly don't understand what the sermon is supposed to be about. The preacher is reading a letter from that Paul fellow who is off being a missionary somewhere, and ... wait, that was kind of provocative, what the preacher just said, about how the clay doesn't get to sass the potter. I wonder what it means?

2. Tell the story of sitting in church in first-century Rome, as an adult who has recently heard of Jesus and has begun coming to these services, kind of eager but knowing so little about this Bible book that other people talk about. The preacher is reading a letter from Paul, who you guess must be someone important. There are a lot of quotations from that Bible book again. Most of this is, frankly, flying right over your head, but you find yourself fascinated by this thing the preacher said about how all Israel is going to be saved.
3. Tell the story of sitting in church in first-century Rome, as an adult who is married to a very active Christian. Well, you're active, too, but not as much. You were raised in a fairly religious home, and you carry around this vague sense of guilt because you probably should know the Bible better, but you don't, and you just don't feel like developing the discipline that daily Bible reading would require. Well, maybe you will, someday. In the meantime, the preacher is reading a letter from that missionary Paul. You want to be interested, at least for your family's sake, but you just don't see what it's about. Except, what was that part the preacher just said about jealousy?

Of course, you don't have to pick the potter and the clay, all Israel being saved, or Paul's desire to make his kinsmen jealous for the gospel. Feel free to select the verses within these three chapters that you hear crying out in your heart for explication, then let that be the text that caught the attention of your first-century congregant.

In any of these instances, you would be letting the members of your congregation "look over the shoulder" of an individual in first-century Rome who is trying to make sense out of a complex passage from the Bible. With a little imagination on your part, this could be quite a humorous presentation, while it would also give you plenty of opportunity for detailed explanation of the meaning of a number of thorny verses. How does that happen? Your chosen character ends up going to ask a friend, "What did it mean, that part where the preacher said...?" The friend rolls his eyes, and then admits he didn't get it, either. The two of them go and ask a third individual, who points out that it makes sense if you remember what it says in this other book of the Bible. Ah, that helps, they say, but what about this other bit? The third one starts to explain, and then sheepishly confesses that she didn't quite get that part herself. So now all three go to ask yet another friend ... you see how much fun this could be.

Any of the longer narratives (such as the exile, the Jacob stories, the book of Judges, and the divided monarchy) can be handled this way, as can other long and involved doctrinal passages.

Exercise 5-3

Select one of the following. Gather together some of the wealth of biblical passages that address the topic you have chosen, some of them complementary, some of them contrasting. Then discern a narrative thread you can use to weave these texts together into a story where we will be able to see how these passages could intersect in a person's life.

1. the theme of holiness in Leviticus
2. justification by grace rather than works, in Galatians and elsewhere
3. the second coming of Jesus
4. the problem of human suffering in Job
5. the recounting of covenantal history in Deuteronomy

With regard to the second coming, for example, you might look at a story line based on John, second-guessing the events that got him exiled to Patmos; or one based on an elder who was feeling rather dreary in the church in Laodicea until the letter got read in worship one Sunday morning; or one that tells about a widow in Thessalonica whose son was a steadfast Christian man just 24 years old when he died, and she finds that she doesn't know what to believe about whether he will be part of life in heaven.

For the theme of holiness in Leviticus, you could look at a person's heartfelt struggle to follow what Leviticus says, with your primary character being someone who desires to love God above all else and yet finds it very hard to put some of the book's requirements into practice: in the time of King David, or in the time of Jesus, or in contemporary society.

The friends of Paul had seen that Paul was journeying into dangerous territory. They pleaded with him to reconsider his plans for Jerusalem. He had answered them, "I am ready not only to be imprisoned but even to die at Jerusalem for the name of the Lord Jesus." They perceived, then, that they would not persuade him not to go. So in the face of this danger they prayerfully set their trust in God: "May the will of the Lord be done."

We pray that same prayer — sometimes by rote, sometimes with a clear-eyed appreciation for the pains and challenges that lie before us: "Thy will be done, on earth as it is in heaven."

There is an undeniable call to courage, then, when we pray such a prayer — may your will be done, O Lord, and if your will leads me to danger or even to death, so be it.

Courage often seems to have this stern and resolute character about it — a resignation that says, "Yes, we will probably die, yet it is our duty and we shall not shirk it." Yet when I look at Paul, eagerly anticipating his opportunity to make a difference for the people of Jerusalem, this acceptance-of-the-likelihood-of-suffering-while-resolutely-pressing-on does not seem to me to tell the entire story. There is this unquenchable joyous conviction in the courage that Paul demonstrated. Paul might well weep while some of his friends were pleading with him and breaking his heart. It might well be that he would die at the hands of other friends when he got to Jerusalem; but maybe, just maybe, this would be the moment when God would slip past the stubbornness of those presently antagonistic friends and convince them that they did not want to continue to kick against the goads any longer, but wanted instead to discover the fullness and wonder of the grace of Christ. "This could be the moment when that is what is going to happen!" — *that* is the unquenchable joyous conviction that moves his soul.

It takes courage to continue, when you see the danger, but it is not the stern-resolution part of the courage that moves Paul along. It is the unquenchable-joyous-conviction part, the recognition that he could be used by God to touch the hearts of these people whom he loved so much.

To speak of unquenchable joy is an odd thing. Any preacher has had plenty of opportunity to discover how severely the human soul can be stifled. You have seen it in the life of others, and you have experienced it when your own soul has been utterly devastated. No one is immune to illness, poverty, or bereavement, and such suffering can easily overwhelm any of us, quenching even the will to live, and certainly washing away any joy from our hearts.

That's why it's important to recognize that unquenchable joyous conviction does not come from a human source. It comes from the decision of Almighty God. Paul knew that. That is why he was able to believe with an unquenchable joyous conviction, even when his friends were telling him that his plans were very dangerous, and even when he himself knew that their perception of the danger was quite right.

It is this unquenchable joyous conviction that explains that line he wrote in the letter to the Romans, putting down his thoughts on paper just before he left Corinth for this trip to Jerusalem, the part where he said, "The gifts and the calling of God are irrevocable" (Romans 11:29). It means that God's love for the children of Israel is forever, unshakable, firm, and resolute no matter what. It means that regarding God's love for Paul himself, as well.

Maybe Paul would live. Maybe he would die. He didn't know how that part was going to turn out. Like Hananiah, Azariah, and Mishael, he knew that God was fully powerful enough to rescue him from the danger, but as to whether or not God would do that, Paul did not know. He did know that the gifts and calling of God are irrevocable. It wasn't a question of how his soul might be trembling at the danger of what might happen to him. It was not up to him to generate courage or joy from within himself, for the unquenchable joyous conviction comes from God, because the gifts and the calling that God had placed in Paul's life are irrevocable.

So Paul would press on, no matter the risk, for the sake of his cousins and his classmates back in Jerusalem.

The depth of his love for those friends is revealed in Romans 9. The plan for taking up the offering to feed the children of Jerusalem is in 2 Corinthians 8 and 9. The scene in the church in Caesarea takes place in Acts 21. The conviction on the irrevocable nature of God's gifts and calling is in Romans 11.

But most of us won't have figured that out. Perhaps we know almost nothing about the Bible; perhaps we know many bits and pieces from here and there. But it's quite unlikely that we will have figured out on our own how these texts interweave. And we probably never will — unless at some point you present us with the narrative line that draws it together for us.

I expect you already know, preacher, that the gifts and the calling of God in your own soul are irrevocable. That can be the source for the unquenchable joyous conviction in your life: an unquenchable joyous conviction just as strong as Paul ever felt.

But it isn't just you, of course, is it? For your congregation and for your community, God's gifts and calling are just as irrevocable for them. What would it be like for them, to know that as the unquenchable joyous conviction in their lives? What would it be like for them, to know — with this unquenchable joyous conviction that comes from God and sustains them even when the circumstances of their lives threaten to blot out every bit of joy — to know that the gifts and the calling of God are irrevocable?

A wise man once said, "How will they hear, without a preacher?"

Fortunately, they have a preacher. They have you.

---

1. Some of the material in this chapter was first published as "The Courage of Conviction" in *Best Sermons 7* (San Francisco: HarperSanFrancisco, 1994), James W. Cox, editor.

2. There really is no substitute for personal daily Bible reading that works through (at least) entire books of the Bible; and by preference, the whole Bible, Genesis to Revelation, every year. Surely we need to encourage our churches to hold this as the corporate expectation for nearly every adult Christian, just as all preachers need to hold this expectation for themselves.

3. Within these chapters one finds both explicit quotations and not-so-obvious citations and allusions, coming from Isaiah, Malachi, Jeremiah, 2 Chronicles, Hosea, Leviticus, Deuteronomy, Joel, Psalms, 1 Samuel, 1 Kings, and Job.

Chapter 6

What Do These Words Mean?

preaching ancient Hebrew and Greek root words as a story

It was taking longer than they expected to fix my car, so I had wandered over to McDonald's and was standing in line there when a couple came in. At first glance, I guessed they were in their late fifties, but I was immediately unsure, because they also looked like they were honeymooners — perhaps not in-their-twenties honeymooners, but with that so-much-in-love look that it made me think maybe they were younger than my first guess.

Sometimes you see a couple of a certain age, and it looks like "happily ever after" for them has come to mean that they are reasonably content in each other's presence. Other couples in that age bracket are still couples — that's no small accomplishment, considering the number of couples-that-were who no longer are — and yet it appears that "happily ever after" for them has come to mean that they have learned to tolerate each other. They have learned to avoid talking about certain topics, in order to keep things on a quiet even keel.

Then every once in a while, maybe at the wedding for one of their grandchildren or at the dinner-dance for someone's retirement, you see a husband and wife who have been married for a long time, and you think, "Wow — they're really in love."

This couple came through the door of McDonald's and it was obvious that they were really in love. Partly it was the laughter in their eyes. Partly it was the mischievous tone of their murmuring conversation. Partly it was the way they were holding hands.

Sometimes you see people holding hands and it looks cute. Sometimes it looks kind of bland. But sometimes people hold hands and from fifteen feet away you can feel the electricity passing between them. As this couple walked over, hand in hand, to get in line behind me, I could feel that electricity moving between them, and it seemed like everyone else did, too. For a moment everyone stopped talking, everyone stopped eating, just to watch this couple as they walked across the lobby.

The man was wearing a grayish beret, with a jaunty tilt to it, so I said, "Nice hat!"

He grinned and said, with a southern accent thick as cornbread batter, "Why, thank you, sir!" And he turned to his wife and said, "See, Ruthie, it *is* a nice hat, the man said so."

She rolled her eyes and shook her head, and she looked at me with *that look*. You know the one I mean, the half-fun half-serious look that says, "Oh my, please don't encourage him."

I've never been too good at placing accents, but there was something in his drawl that I thought maybe I'd heard before, so I took a chance and guessed, "South Carolina?"

He shook his head. "No," he said, "but you're close. We're from Georgia."

I stuck out my hand and said, "Welcome to Kansas." And that's how I got to eat lunch with Ruth and Cameron Hall.

They were just touring around, they said, driving a rather zigzag course on their way to the west coast. They were going to see Mount Rushmore, in a few days, but they also wanted to see some of the small towns of the great plains. It's the kind of trip they'd always said they wanted to take, all throughout 54 years of marriage, and they were finally doing it. I said there must be some mistake because if they'd been married 54 years, that would mean Ruth couldn't have been more than four or five on her wedding day, and I didn't think you could get married that young even in Georgia.

No, she laughed, they were childhood sweethearts, but it wasn't quite that soon. Cameron was three years ahead of her in school. He graduated and went into the army, and then, when he came home from the war, he was 21 and she had turned 18, and they got married six days later.

Cameron shook his head in wonder as he said, "They wanted to take *three whole weeks* to make lots of wedding plans and all, but I told them I didn't think I could last that long. Even six days seemed like forever."

She laughed and squeezed him on the arm, and she did that little shake of her head that every teenage girl learns, the one that makes her hair flip from side to side, and in that moment somehow I could see what she must have looked like when she was eighteen. She teased him, "You didn't seem to be any the worse for the delay, dear. And some would say that what you got was worth waiting those six days for."

I said it was obvious that being in love had kept them young, that I had guessed that they were in their late fifties. I'd be willing to concede maybe early sixties, but I would not have guessed 72 and 75.

It is always a heartwarming thing, when you encounter a story of a love so steady and strong, so pure and passionate, that it would keep on burning bright even during times of great trial, like Cameron and Ruth during those three anxious teenage years of separation during the Second World War. But it was a wondrously astonishing thing, to see a couple with a love burning so bright after 54 years of marriage that they could turn heads when they walked into a McDonald's, and everyone who sees them thinks, "Wow, I want to be in love like that."

Some of the very best stories close with the line, "And they lived happily ever after." Perhaps, though, it is only in fairy tales that stories go that way. As you are aware, preacher, many of those gathering in the sanctuary this Sunday will be realizing that "happily ever after" isn't happening too well for them.

On the days when our lives are feeling blue or aggravated or surly, we might well settle for "adequately ever after" if we could just figure out how to get there. It might be bland. It might be boring. Still — if "happily ever after" means that we would learn to be content and companionable, that we would get to the point where we squabble less often, that we would feel a mild-yet-sustaining sense of warmth and affection — if "happily ever after" means "adequately ever after" or "comfortably ever after" or something along those lines — then that could be pretty good, all things considered.

But what if that isn't what "happily ever after" actually is supposed to mean? What if "happily ever after" means something more than that? What if "happily ever after" is just the eye-rolling grin children-are-present-but-you-know-what-I'm-really-talking-about acknowledgment of an electricity that keeps on simmering just under the surface? What if "passionately ever after" is what it really means?

Any movie theater advertising promotion, any grocery store checkout magazine rack can tell you about how passion can be intensely passionate, right now. But what if you want to find out about a passion that can keep on being passionate for the long term? Everybody knows that it is possible to feel a strong sense of desire and devotion and delight, right now. But will we still feel that way ever after? What would it be like to live passionately ever after?

Is it possible to be in love like that? Passionately ever after?

God is in love like that.

God is passionately in love. Passionately in love with us right now, and passionately in love for the long term. God intends for us to live passionately ever after.

As a young soldier just back from World War II, there was this feeling of intense enthusiastic desire that Cameron was referring to when he allowed as how, after three years of separation because of the war, even six more days seemed like a very long time to wait. I could tell that he was partly making fun of himself and partly still sympathizing with himself as that 21-year-old boy, so eager to make love with his new bride. Of course, while we were sitting there at lunch, neither Cameron nor Ruth used words like "sex" or "making love" or any such term as that. Surely it would have been embarrassing for all three of us if they had. And yet, even though nobody actually said it, all three of us knew that that was what we were talking about.

There are certain concepts that are rooted so deeply in the heritage of God's people that they developed particular words for them. Preachers learn these words; you have probably learned quite a few of them by now: words like *hesed* and *berith*, *agape* and *metanoia*. You have probably also learned that the point of knowing these words is not so that you can have an impressive vocabulary of key Greek and Hebrew terms; rather, these words are worth knowing because they help you to know the heritage. Knowing these words helps you know the experiences and the stories that shape our faith.

Take *hesed*, for example: covenant faithfulness. The term is translated as *lovingkindness* or *steadfast love* in various translations. The idea is fairly simple: When you make a covenant, you need to be faithful to that covenant. In its most basic form, it simply declares that you must keep your promises. Yet there is more to it than this basic form, for covenant faithfulness does not aim simply for determined-yet-reluctant obedience. I could do my duty simply because I must, but *hesed* calls me to fulfill what I have pledged because I am glad to establish my love that way.

Now if you have learned *hesed* as a vocabulary term, it equips you to understand stacks of Bible passages. Psalm 136 is the obvious example: a 26-fold repetition of the phrase "his *hesed* endures forever," as an unquenchable joyous line-by-line refrain as we recite what God has done in the history of our people. The term itself, along with its steady repetition, reminds us constantly that when we are talking about God's covenant faithfulness, we are talking about the fact that God will fulfill in gladness and love what God has declared. As we have seen this again and again in the past, so shall we live in confidence through all the days to come.

When you learn a vocabulary word like this one, you gain a powerful term for understanding what the love of God is like. And then, as a preacher, you want this for your congregation, too. You want them also to develop a biblical vocabulary, so that they can gain that same understanding.

And what happens next? You discover that the congregation does not get really excited about a sermon that offers a vocabulary lesson. Sermons about Hebrew and Greek root words are famous for how boring everyone finds them.

In order to help your congregation get hold of these root words, then, you need to start not with the vocabulary, but with stories.

Recount to us the biblical narratives that have given those powerful words their power. Tell us a story or a parable that will enable us to see and feel what these words really mean. Rather than explain what *hesed* means in ancient Hebrew, show us God's covenant faithfulness to Abram the ancient Hebrew (and then you can note that God's covenant faithfulness got put into an ancient Hebrew word, *hesed*, which you might just use from time to time in the rest of the sermon, and in days to come, as shorthand for God's covenant faithfulness not just to ancient Hebrews, but to us today as well).

For most of the key biblical terms, that actually turns out to be fairly easy. The only one that is kind of tricky is *qannah*, because most of us are at least a little embarrassed when it comes to talking about sex.

Without saying it in direct speech, Cameron indicated — when he grinned and said that six days seemed like forever — that he was feeling a pretty powerful emotion, during those days of waiting for the wedding. Without saying it in direct speech, Ruth indicated — when she did the little head shake and noted that what he got was worth waiting for — that she was feeling a pretty powerful emotion as well. That emotion they were feeling was *qannah*: They were feeling eager and passionate about each other. It was clear that Cameron and Ruth continued to feel this very same way about each other many decades later. They shared a *qannah* that was strong and vibrant (even though they did not and surely would not talk about this *qannah* in anything other than a playful allusion with someone they had just met while standing in line in a fast-food restaurant).

This is how God feels about us. Our God is a passionate God. The love with which God loves us is a passionate love — full of eager longing, ardent and passionate even across the long span of years.

Hmmm. Although passion is a sexy word — indeed, *because* passion is a sexy word — it is hard to preach it where children (and adults) may be present. Chapter 3 points out one danger — although the excitement of human sexuality may well serve as a powerful analogue of the passion of God's love for us, saying so within a sermon might not get the grown-ups thinking about the love of God, but only thinking (again) about sex. But what about the kids? Picture one of the congregation's extended families meeting after church for Sunday dinner in their favorite restaurant, and as the waitress stands ready to take orders, one of the children pipes up, "Mommy, what did that mean, when the preacher said God is eager to love us, like the bride and bridegroom eager to make love with each other?" Wouldn't that be an intriguing scenario, there in the restaurant, with the grandmother and the aunts and the uncles and all the other children all gathered around? It would give us several fascinating questions to ponder. We might wonder, first of all, just how Mommy will answer that. We might consider, second, how the church elders might decide to discuss such sermon topics with the preacher. We might ask, third, how any preacher would ever be brave or foolish enough to say it, to give us the opportunity to consider those first two questions.

The translators of the Bible were not brave or foolish enough to be quite that explicit when they addressed themselves to translating *qannah* into English. They might indeed have said that our God is a passionate God, who loves us with deep and enduring passion (that is, with eager longing like newlyweds eager to consummate their love as they establish a relationship that will endure passionately ever after). Wouldn't that be an intriguing scenario, if they had been that direct in their translation work? Would we have ended up with children of every generation asking, "Mommy, what does that mean, when the Bible says God loves us passionately?"

You can see how that question, from all those children down the generations, might have embarrassed a lot of mothers (and Sunday school teachers, and even preachers). It would nevertheless have created a multitude of opportunities for the youngsters to gain insight into just how powerful God's love for us is. As it has turned out, though, all those opportunities have not come about, for those who have translated the Bible into English have generally not been either brave or foolish enough to tell us what *qannah* means.

Instead, they have given us two terms. These terms are not wrong, precisely, but they do not point us straight down the path. When *qannah* shows up in adjective form, the translators have given us *zealous* and *jealous* as translations. When it shows up as a noun, the translators have opted for *zeal* or *jealousy*.

You can see how it works, readily enough. If I have a passion for baseball or for jazz or for baklava or for woodworking, you would not be wrong if you said I have a zeal for such things. Still, it seems like a bland way of saying it.

On the other hand, if I am deeply in love with you and some third party tries to come elbowing in, I will not be indifferent about this. It would not be incorrect to suggest that I will be jealous (especially if you start making eyes at that interloper). But to focus on the jealousy is to begin noticing and commenting at the middle of the story, ignoring where it came from. If I didn't care about you, it would not matter to me who you make eyes at, but if I love you passionately, I will respond quite vividly. Great passion and great provocation will lead to great jealousy.

Now because you read your (English) Bible regularly, preacher, you have probably noted some of the texts that the translators have given us, with passages that speak of the zeal of the Lord, or that teach us that our God is a jealous God. What those translators have given you is not false. But they haven't told you everything that you ought to know about what those texts are saying about the passionate love of God. They have not been quite brave or foolish enough to say it.

Yet those who wrote the original Hebrew text of the Bible *were* brave and foolish enough to say it — to tell us that our God feels passionate about his people.

Most English translations of Deuteronomy 4:24, for example, give us something like this: "The Lord your God is a blazing fire; he is a jealous God." Suppose, though, we give the Hebrew term *qannah* permission to tell us something a little stronger, and listen to the scripture as it declares: "The Lord your God is a blazing fire; he is a passionate God." Do we hear the word of the Lord a little bit differently, if we do that?

How about in the Ten Commandments? If you memorized the second commandment, you learned the phrase that says, "I, the Lord your God, am a jealous God." The second commandment is about graven images and idols. It instructs us that we are not to make them and we are not to worship them. God will not be pleased if we should decide to give our love to another, offering our worship to something made by human hands. God will indeed be jealous and angry if we do that. It *is* about jealousy, right there. Yet it appears likely to me that we would get the point better if we had memorized this commandment to include the phrase, "I, the Lord your God, am a passionate God." We would understand that the love of God for us is passionate rather than platonic, which would then mean, as the remainder of the second commandment goes on to indicate, that God will not be indifferent or philosophical about it when we turn from our ardent love for him, in order to worship and serve the creature rather than the creator.

Twenty-seven centuries ago a young man named Isaiah lived in Jerusalem. He saw a vision of the intense passionate love of God. It would not be passionate just for a few weeks or months. The intense passionate love of God would be passionate for decades, for centuries, for ever.

So Isaiah wrote it down, and it became part of the Bible. It is a part of the Bible that we usually read around Christmas. In his vision, Isaiah saw that people would rejoice in the intense passionate love of God. It would be like people rejoicing at the harvest, like a great passionate thanksgiving feast after many months on short rations, not knowing if the food would hold out until harvest time. It would be like people when the war was won, like a great passionate homecoming of soldiers who endured the horrors of the battlefield, not knowing if they would survive, not knowing if they would ever see their loved ones again (Isaiah 9:2-7).

Isaiah saw his vision around the year we now call 740 BC. At that point, all of the events of his vision would take place far in the future. The people who listened to Isaiah would have to wait a long time, for the glory of the Lord to be fulfilled. The glory of the Lord would be fulfilled, but it would be far beyond their own lifetimes. Would it be worth it, waiting for the glory of God, believing in the glory of God, when you knew it would not happen in your generation, or in the generation of your children or grandchildren? Would that be worth it? Isaiah thought so. He urged his people to wait for the glory of God to be revealed.

If you were one of those people, listening to Isaiah's urgent admonitions, you might feel pretty skeptical about the whole thing. Here comes Isaiah, talking about glorious events that are going to happen many generations from now, but what makes him think he actually *knows*? Everybody has experienced this, too many times to count. You have firmly scheduled something for tomorrow or next week, and you know that this is what you are going to do; then some unexpected event takes place and throws everything off-kilter. If a person can't even predict next month with full accuracy, how can you possibly suppose you *know* something about what God will be up to ten or twenty generations into the future?

Yet when Isaiah saw it, he saw it with intense clarity. He felt such certainty in his heart that when he wrote it down, he did something quite interesting.

All of the events he recounted were in the distant future for him, but as he wrote down what he had seen, he reported several of the events as if they had already happened. The people have seen a great light; God has shattered the power of their oppressors. Other details are written in the present tense: Unto us a child is born, unto us a son is given. And some of the material looks still further into the future: The government will be on his shoulders, he will reign on David's throne.

In Isaiah's day it was all in the future, yet he saw it so vividly that he could step across a great span of time — a seven-century span of time, as it turns out — as he stepped into the middle of the picture, to a spot where he could tell some of it as what's already happened, some as what's happening now, and some that will still be in the future when the first part has come true.

He stepped into the vision to the moment when what's happening now is the birth of the Son. Who is this Son who is born to us? Isaiah indicates that this Son has four names.[1] He is named Wonderful Counselor, Mighty God, Everlasting Father, and Prince of Peace. In John 14:26 and elsewhere, one of the words used to identify the Holy Spirit is the παρακλητης — the Comforter or Advocate — the Counselor — Wonderful Counselor. If Jesus is the Prince of Peace, and if the Everlasting Father is our Father who art in heaven, to whom Jesus prayed and taught us to pray, then we have Jesus, the Spirit, and the Father, the three persons of the Trinity. A Son has been born for us. This Son is the incarnation of the Mighty God who is Wonderful Counselor, Everlasting Father, and the Prince of Peace. It is not as if God became triune at the moment of the incarnation, or became triune when early Christian writers developed the term Trinity.[2] Rather, the Mighty God who eternally is Wonderful Counselor, Everlasting Father, Prince of Peace — who forever has been Father, Son, and Spirit — becomes incarnate *for us* in the birth of the Son. This means that in the human presence of Jesus we can and genuinely do encounter God with us — Emmanuel (Isaiah 7:14, cited in Matthew 1:22-23) — all of the fullness of God dwelling in human form, coming to establish and uphold the justice and righteousness of our God, within our hearts.

These things will happen, Isaiah tells us, they will happen in this Son who is born for us. Why will these things happen? What will make all this happen? The answer comes in the last line of the reading — the zeal of the Lord Almighty will accomplish this.

How about that word *zeal*? It's that Hebrew term *qannah* again. What it means is, the passion of the Lord Almighty will accomplish this. God's passionate love, the intense enthusiastic desire of the Lord Almighty for the redemption of all the world, that will be established at the particular point in time when to us a Son is born: The Son who would be the incarnation of the Mighty God who is Everlasting Father, Wonderful Counselor, and the Prince of Peace.

Exercise 6-1

Choose one of the following vocabulary terms. Take the time to do a fairly deep search on that term, using the standard concordances, dictionaries, computer resources, and other exegetical tools. Trace the term's usage across the biblical literature, so that it becomes part of the way you understand the message of the Bible.

1. *hesed*: covenant faithfulness
2. *berith/diatheke*: covenant
3. *eschaton*: the last things
4. *ruach/pneuma*: spirit/breath/wind

5. *basileia theou*: kingdom of God
6. *shekinah*: glory
7. *kapporeth/hilasterion*: the mercy seat
8. *agape*: the love of God
9. *berakah/eulogia*: blessing
10. *rebed yahweh/pais theou*: servant of God
11. *shalom/irene*: peace
12. *metanoia*: repentance

Now consider how to use that knowledge within a narrative that you would present as a sermon to your congregation.

1. Tell the story of a major Bible character — Abraham, Moses, Ezekiel, Paul, John — letting that term form a theme in the background that gives light to the action of the story. For example, tell us what it is like for Abram, cutting a covenant with God in Genesis 15. Or let us come along with Ezekiel as he muses on whether God's covenant faithfulness really does endure forever. Or show us Saul of Tarsus as a schoolboy learning about the *kapporeth*, and then let us see him in later life as Paul the apostle, recognizing that God has now established Jesus as the *hilasterion*.
2. Tell the story of a less-well-known Bible character — Aaron, Ruth, Tychicus, Miriam, Andrew — letting that term form a theme in the background that gives light to the action of the story. For example, show us Ruth or Miriam as she struggles with the difficulty of what it can mean that through Abraham all the nations will experience the blessing of God.
3. Tell the story of a Christian in New Testament times — a frazzled young mother in Rome, a lonely old man in Antioch, a pregnant engaged couple in Corinth — letting that term form a theme in the background that gives light to the action of the story. For example, let us listen in on the conversation of that young couple as they consider what decisions they should make, in the light of the *eschaton*.

4. Tell the story of an interesting character you create — an immigrant restaurant worker in an ethnic neighborhood in a large American city during the 1930s; an office worker who has become aware that the way the boss is running the business is not in compliance with the law; a man who left his wife and three children five years ago and moved across the country to start a new life, who has now found that in spite of his new job and string of girlfriends he keeps feeling homesick, and he keeps wondering whether it ever would be possible to go back and restore his relationships with the family he left behind — letting that term form a theme in the background that gives light to the action of the story. For any of these three, for example, show us how they discover what *shalom* is about.
5. Tell the story of someone you have known — a teacher from elementary school days, the boss you worked for in college, your friend's nephew who got busted for marijuana possession — letting that term form a theme in the background that gives light to the action of the story. For example, you might show us that although we see the wind's effect the moment it moves the branches in the trees, we still can't see the wind before it moves the branches or afterward (thus we don't know where it comes from or where it is going). So although we may well perceive what the Spirit of God was doing at one moment in the life of the teacher (or the boss or the nephew), we mostly won't be able to describe just what the Spirit was up to on the way to that moment, nor will we be able to say how the Spirit will go about bringing further results in the time to come.

I leaned my elbows on the table, there at McDonald's, and asked Ruth and Cameron Hall, "How do you do this? How have you stayed so in love, all these years?" They looked at me as if this was a strange question. They turned toward each other with this "how do we answer this" look on their faces. Then their eyes met, and they exchanged a glance. I can't describe this glance — they did not wink or grin or make any particular facial gestures. They did not speak. The length of this glance was surely no longer than two seconds, but in those two seconds, this glance they exchanged had so much passion and connection in it that it almost made me cry. And in my soul, I did cry, "Oh! When I grow up, I want to be in love like that!"

Then they turned back to me, and Cameron said, "I don't think we have. Stayed in love, that is. That would be like love is a place you stay. But love is more like a walk. You take steps. Every day we take steps to put our love into words and into actions. To love each other a little more, every day."

God's love for us is like that.

Every day — for centuries and centuries — forever. We don't stay in love. Love is more like a walk, where every day you take steps to put your love for God into words and into actions, so that the passion burns ever brighter. Our God is a flaming fire: a passionate God!

Sometimes we have to wait, and it seems like a very long time indeed. Some of the attainment of that full and passionate love will not come until some point in the future. It's hard to wait for the glory of God to be fulfilled in us, but fulfilled it shall be. Because the last line of the story is: "And they all lived passionately ever after."

---

1. We should count ourselves fortunate that the names given in Isaiah 9 are less obscure and cumbersome than the name Isaiah gave his own son in Isaiah 8. One can only wonder at how young Mahershalalhashbaz's friends must have teased him on the playground when he was in fourth grade.

2. The first extant use of the term appears to come from Theophilus of Antioch (ca 180), *Of the Fourth Day*, chapter 15. Clement of Alexandria (ca 190), uses the term as well, *Stromata* 5:14. An extended argument on the nature of the Trinity can be found in Tertullian (ca 200), *Against Praxeas*, in chapters 2, 9, 11, and elsewhere.

Chapter 7

Once Before There Was A Time

preaching the doctrine of predestination as a story

Once upon a time there was a handsome prince. Ever since he was a small boy he had known that his parents had selected a princess for him to marry. At times he thought he should be grateful. His parents' thoughtfulness meant that he was spared all that teenage boy awkwardness about girls and dating and all that, but somehow he didn't feel grateful.

His parents explained, kindly and patiently, that he was indeed destined to marry the princess, according to the arrangement they had worked out with her parents, the king and queen of a far country. But they also said that it would be up to him to decide. He did not understand how both of those could be true, but he took comfort in the promise that he would have the power to say, "No."

The day came when the princess arrived at the castle, after a caravan journey of many days from the far country that was her homeland. The prince hid in a corner of one of the balconies, as the caravan rode into the courtyard. He watched and listened to their conversation and he discovered that the princess was beautiful and lively and witty and intelligent. He could hear the compassion in her voice as she gave instructions to the servants. He thought he could detect a hint of nervousness in her laugh. Yet, that same laughter also revealed something, some deep inner joy it seemed, and that joy somehow reached over the balcony rail and touched the ache in his own heart.

Nevertheless, he was determined that he would make his own decision.

Later that day, the prince and the princess were formally introduced in the grand ballroom of the castle. She had never seen him before, of course, and yet she looked and spoke in ways that indicated she was very much in love with him. On this day of meeting she gave him a single perfect rose, which she said symbolized the ardor and the fullness of her love for him. Soft gasps of wonder and delight burst from all the courtiers standing around watching. What a fine gift she had offered to him!

Yet, with an air of dismissal and boredom, the prince tossed the flower aside onto a table. He looked around the ballroom at all the gathered nobles. He did not bother to look at the princess as he declared, in his public proclamation voice, "I will marry whom I want to, when I want to."

Just like that, the prince's slap-in-the-face boorishness dispelled all the cheery warmth the princess had inspired — but she was not flustered. She nodded her head, probably not more than a few inches, and yet with such graciousness that it seemed to be a deep and humble curtsey. Then she smiled at him — a radiant smile, with her eyes and cheeks and mouth all smiling, a smile like May sunlight on a meadow of wildflowers. In her voice you could hear the warmth of springtime melting away the bitter cold of winter as she said, "Indeed you shall, your highness, I have no doubt of it."

Her answer pleased everyone — except for the prince. It made him mad, and he stormed out of the room.

How would the princess respond to all this? Some of the courtiers quietly voiced their opinions to one another, "If the prince continues to behave this way, she will soon tire of his rudeness, and will order her attendants to make ready for the return to her homeland."

The prince did continue to behave this way, but the princess did not give up so easily as the nobles had guessed. Day by day she would greet him with a cheery, "Good morning" at breakfast. She kept bumping into him, coming around corners in the hallways, smiling at him with those incredible eyes, and asking if he would care to go for a walk in the gardens. Sometimes he was frostily polite, and sometimes he made rude comments. Sometimes he walked past as if she weren't there. But she was persistent, and very much in love.

And then one day —

One of the most fascinating developments in all the history of doctrine is the way Calvinism evolved over time. (Granted, it doesn't take all that much to be one of the most fascinating developments in the history of doctrine.) John Calvin discerned, as few have, what it means to build a systematic understanding of the message of God, taking into account the variety and complexity of that message, and then to present that systematic understanding clearly enough that ordinary people can follow more of that complexity than they previously could grasp. He gave us a model that all pastors would want to emulate, as they endeavor to answer those persistent questions that people have asked in every parish.

Alas, doctrine is not a hot topic for most Christians these days; the history of doctrine, even less so. Doctrinal sermons were once a well-respected tool in the preacher's satchel. They provided the opportunity for the minister to explain how a variety of relevant texts come together to form a systematic understanding of a topic of interest to Christians — the atonement, sanctification, eternal life, and prayer. Parishioners wanted to gain a systematic understanding of these things. They attended religiously, they took notes, they read and pondered the passages of scripture for the upcoming sermon, they asked further questions afterward.

That no longer seems to be the case among those who come to church quite regularly. If you ask, you could probably find a few brave souls in most any congregation who would be glad to listen to a carefully outlined exposition of doctrine from the pulpit, but you would also find that the large majority of the membership would look rather queasy at the prospect. And if that's how the most faithful would feel, then it is very hard to imagine that explanations of Christian doctrine will be the means of preaching the gospel to the world that does not presently come to church.

Still, as a preacher you must teach doctrine to your congregation. Doing so in lecture style will often not be the most effective, in our present culture. If, instead, you present doctrine in narrative style, many people will gain a much more comprehensive understanding of the Christian faith than they ever had before. By itself, of course, that will not tell them everything they need to know. Sermons never do. When people want to push themselves to learn as much about a topic as they can, they have to devote a substantial amount of time to reading and pondering the material, and discussing it with others. A church's program can provide people numerous opportunities for such study. A sermon can provide people motivation for such study, but the sermon itself cannot be that study.

That presents you with this fact, preacher: You must teach doctrine to your congregation, yet no sermon can possibly tell them everything they need to know about any doctrine. Since you can't tell them everything they need to know anyway, a sermon that tries to present the most possible information will still be insufficient. A sermon that tells a story, on the other hand, can prove to be a very useful means of enabling people to get a rudimentary-yet-valid grasp on doctrine, in a way that can motivate them to want to study more. These next chapters provide some instruction and exercises to help you craft such sermons.

Before you can preach a sermon on a given doctrine, however, you yourself need to be clear about the doctrine in question. Let me take Calvinism, as a convenient example. It is the long-standing heritage of the Presbyterian and Reformed traditions, yet most members of Presbyterian or Reformed churches no longer study it or understand it. As for people in other denominations, at most they will "know" only one thing about Calvinism, namely that Calvinism teaches that God has predestined some people for salvation and others for damnation.

One of the things we might learn from studying the history of doctrine is that there are some differences between what Calvin taught and what followers of Calvin later taught. To say "Calvinism equals predestination" would be an oversimplification at any point in the tradition. Yet as the doctrine evolved, this became more accurate in the generations following Calvin than it was in Calvin himself.

It is worth noting, for example, that when Calvin presented his thinking in its most systematic fashion (in the 1559 edition of the *Institutes of the Christian Religion*), he did not address himself specifically to the question of predestination until book 3, chapters 21 to 24. He discussed dozens of other topics first (for example, book 3, chapter 19 is about Christian liberty; chapter 20 is about prayer). This makes it quite difficult to argue that predestination was the first thing Calvin wanted to talk about.

Although B. A. Gerrish's recent study, *Grace and Gratitude: the Eucharistic Theology of John Calvin*,[1] is primarily an exposition to Calvin's doctrine of the Lord's Supper, it can also serve as a fine introduction to Calvin's overall style of thinking. Indeed, as a pair of words to summarize Calvin's thinking, *grace* and *gratitude* express well his conviction that all the gifts of life and redemption are given as free acts of divine grace, and the proper human response, from which all true piety then emerges, is gratitude. Two words cannot tell you everything you need to know (I am going to suggest a third term in just a moment), but already *grace* and *gratitude* come far closer to providing a true picture of Calvin's thinking than the word *predestination* does.

If it is fair to say that Calvin's doctrine of redemption was a doctrine of grace and his doctrine of the Christian life was a doctrine of gratitude, we might also say that Calvin's epistemology — his doctrine of how we know the things we know — was an epistemology of *revelation*. How do we know what to believe about God and salvation and life? We find out about these things by reading the Bible, and learning what God has revealed there. This comes out clearly in the following passage, where Calvin was beginning an exploration of some of the thorny texts in Romans chapter 9:

> *The predestination of God is truly a labyrinth from which the mind of man is wholly incapable of extricating itself. But the curiosity of man is so insistent that the more dangerous it is to inquire into a subject, the more boldly he rushes to do so. Thus when predestination is being discussed, because he cannot keep himself within proper limits, he immediately plunges into the depths of the sea by his impetuosity. What remedy then will there be for the godly? Must they avoid every thought of predestination? Not at all. Since the Holy Spirit has taught us nothing but what it is to our interest to know, this knowledge will undoubtedly be useful to us, provided we shall confine it to the Word of God. Let this, therefore, be our sacred rule, not to seek to*

> *know anything about it except what Scripture teaches us. Where the Lord closes His holy mouth, let us also stop our minds from going on further.*[2]

The human mind has its limits. When we try to reason our way outside those limits, our finitude and our fallibility mean that we cannot trust the answers we come up with. We will postulate inadequate answers because of our incomplete information and ability; we will postulate self-serving answers because of our sinfulness. Thus, if we are wise and faithful, we will seek to find the answers we need in scripture, not in speculation.

"I like to think of God," said Freddy, "as a kind and benevolent grandfather. He knows us, and loves us; and even though we get it wrong a lot of the time, he'll always just shake his head and chuckle and keep on loving us."

Suzanne had a different perspective. "I like to think of God," she said, "as a vast ocean of love, which surrounds us always. It buoys us up in our best moments and when life overwhelms us so that we are drowning in sorrows, what better place is there to drown than in the ocean of God's love?"

If Calvin were given the opportunity to respond to these contemporary ideas, he would probably say something like this: "Why should anyone — why would even you yourselves — care about how you like to imagine what God is like? No one can know anything, by speculating about how they would *like to think* of God! The limits of the human mind mean that we could never claim to know everything about God, but if we want to *know* anything at all — instead of just making things up, according to our own preferences — we must learn it by reading what God has revealed to us in the scriptures."

As for the doctrine of predestination, Calvin believed it in an exacting way. Before the creation of the world, God chose some people for salvation and others for damnation, and that was that. The only possible justification for this doctrine is that this is what the Bible, taken as a whole, teaches us. (Indeed, that's the only possible justification for any doctrine.) Calvin believed that he had learned this doctrine of predestination from scripture, but he was mistaken about that, as we shall see.

Calvin's reasoning went like this: Sovereignty means that God's will always comes to pass. When God makes a decision, that's the way things happen, so when the sovereign Lord decides to save someone, that person will be saved. Saving someone means forgiving them for their sins, and transforming their behavior so that the visible marks of the Christian life become more and more established there. But when you look around, you don't see that happening with everyone. You see some people who evidence Christian joy and confidence, repentance and discipline, and it's clear that God has called them and is transforming them into saints. You see other people who don't look like that at all. They have no interest in devotion or virtue, but only in their own pleasures and ambitions. Now if God had decided to save those latter individuals, it would have worked better than that. The transforming power of God would be just as visible in their lives as it is in the lives of those saints-in-process we noticed a minute ago. But if God hasn't decided to save them, then they are lost — for all of humanity is lost in sin, none of us can save ourselves. Moreover, God has made all such decisions from before the foundation of the earth, which means God decided from eternity to create humanity with the intention of saving some and not saving others. Thus within the eternal counsel of God, the elect have been created for redemption, and the reprobate have been created for damnation. To God be all the glory.

This gives us a picture of a loving God who has created billions of people who are fated to inevitable eternal damnation. Isn't that a puzzling picture? It is hard to say what it means that God so loves the world, and as sovereign Lord has determined that the large majority of the world shall be condemned to hell.[3]

Many Calvinists have demurred from saying it quite this way. It is not so much that God *determined* that the damned would be damned, they would argue. God created humanity; all have sinned; none of us can be saved by our own efforts or merits. Consider then, the sovereign Lord is under no *obligation* to save anyone. Nevertheless, with astonishing graciousness this loving heavenly Father has decided to save some of those who otherwise would be lost, forever without hope. Is not this indeed something that should move our hearts to earnest thanksgiving?

Many a heartfelt Calvinist has tried to say it that way. But when they do, they often find that they end up with a troubled understanding of the love of God.

Once upon a time, a crew of teenagers went on a field trip. They wandered off the path, and all of them fell into the quicksand. Some panicked, crying for help; some thought that they were going to make it to safety, so they concentrated their efforts on extricating themselves; still others thought that they were going to make it to safety, and they mocked those who were pleading for help.

But the quicksand was more treacherous than they knew. Those who imagined they would work their way out of it were mistaken; no matter how thoughtful and patient and careful their motions were, they inevitably sank further in, and they edged closer and closer to drowning. Those who were panicking and yelling in the hope that someone would come and rescue them were also mistaken, for none of their friends could rescue them. Indeed, no one in the whole world could rescue them.

No one, that is, except for the park ranger.

And indeed, the park ranger came along at just the right time. He looked around, and saw all these teenagers trapped in the quicksand. Foolish teens! Why didn't you stay in the areas that were marked as safe? The park ranger shook his head. Surely all of them deserved to die for straying outside the proper boundaries. If he let them die, they would merely be receiving the consequences of their own poor choice of wandering off the path.

Ah, but this was the park ranger, after all. It was for the sake of rescuing teenagers trapped in quicksand that he became a park ranger. As he looked around, he picked out various ones. There was no discernible pattern to the way he chose. Some of those whom he selected were kind or pretty or smart or strong or virtuous. But many were not. Most were just average. He just — chose. Those whom he rescued were rescued, and those whom he did not rescue were left to drown.

Do note — it was not because of lack of ability or time or resources. The park ranger has always had enough skill and enough rope to rescue an infinite number of teenagers drowning in quicksand. The park ranger could have rescued them all, but that's not what he decided to do. Instead, he chose to rescue some of them, and those were the ones he pulled out of the muck and mire, so that he could set their feet on firm ground once again.

Well, as you might imagine, it made the news. I watched it on television. The reporter asked, "Why did you rescue these teenagers?"

The park ranger answered, "Because I love them. Indeed, I love all the teenagers, even though they sometimes do make bad choices and put themselves in very troubling situations. I love all the teenagers in the world. That's why I became a park ranger, so that I could rescue them in their time of deep distress."

The reporter hesitated for a moment, and then she asked, "But if you love all the teenagers, if it is your love that moved you to rescue them, why then did you choose to rescue some and not others?"

I was very curious to hear how the park ranger might respond to that question. But alas, that's when the television anchorman broke in. He was obviously a man with theological training; he knew he needed to offer his own wise commentary, and then break for a commercial. He told us, "The point to focus on, then, is that some were rescued, and we should be grateful for this." Then the picture cut to rapid-fire images of happy teenagers serving hamburgers at a fast-food restaurant. I reflected on all this for a few moments. The message touched me deep inside, so I went out to buy lunch at their restaurant.

A friend told me later about a follow-up program he had seen on another channel. It was an interview with the mother of one of the girls who had drowned in the quicksand. The mother was quite heartbroken, my friend told me; it was obvious that she loved her daughter very much. She kept asking one of those unanswerable questions: "If the park ranger became the park ranger because of his love for all the teenagers in the world, why wouldn't he love my daughter at least as much as I do?"

Calvin's logic led him inexorably to the stark conclusion that the sovereign God had created the world, choosing some for heaven and others for hell. It is a measure of the courage of Calvin's conviction that he did not endeavor to soften this conclusion. Having committed himself to this doctrine of absolute sovereignty, Calvin did not try to pretend that God was not in charge of who is saved and who is damned. God chose. Some are saved, and some are damned, because that's what God chose. Let us offer our thanks and praise that God chose to save some.

Why did God choose to do it this way? This is not a matter for human knowledge, Calvin insisted; this took place by the secret counsel and decision of God. Calvin had no further explanation to offer, other than to say that the ways of God are inscrutable. Let not the creation argue against the ways of its Creator. Yet even if we can silence our objections, even if we can in quiet reverence accept Calvin's admonition, that still leaves us quite uncertain as to what the doctrine of the love of God means. We can say that God loves the world, yet what does that mean, if God has chosen for most of the world to be damned? We can say that God loved the world so much that he sent his Son into the world not to condemn the world but to save the world through him. Yet what does that mean if God had already decided before creating the world that most of that world would irrevocably be condemned to hell?

Perhaps this is clearest if we individualize it. Take the case of Uncle Mort, a lovable old rascal, with plenty of faults and no use for religion. If Uncle Mort is one of the damned, that means that God loves Uncle Mort, and yet wants him to be damned. What are we to make of this notion? We love Uncle Mort, and long for him to be saved. Would that mean, then, that we love Uncle Mort more than God does?

These uncomfortable questions arise from Calvin's assessment of predestination. If we take a closer look at the premises and conclusions in Calvin's reasoning, we will see where some of the problems come from.

1. Sovereignty means that God's will always comes to pass. When God makes a decision, that's the way things happen, so when the sovereign Lord decides to save someone, that person will be saved.

2. Saving someone means forgiving them for their sins, and transforming their behavior so that the visible marks of the Christian life become more and more established there.
3. When you look around, you don't see that happening with everyone. You see some people who evidence Christian joy and confidence, repentance and discipline. It's clear that God has called them and is transforming them into saints. You see other people who don't look like that at all. They have no interest in devotion or virtue, but only in their own pleasures and ambitions.
4. If God had decided to save those latter individuals, it would have worked better than that. The transforming power of God would be just as visible in their lives as it is in the lives of those saints we noticed.
5. If God hasn't decided to save them, then they are lost — for all of humanity is lost in sin, none of us can save ourselves.
6. Moreover, God has made all such decisions from before the foundation of the earth, which means that God decided from eternity to create humanity with the intention of saving some and not saving others. Thus within the eternal counsel of God, the elect have been created for redemption, and the reprobate have been created for damnation.

Shouldn't we notice a problem with premise 1? Do we know that God's will always comes to pass? We could assume that as self-evident, yet we frequently see, in scripture and in our own hearts, that the will of God is rejected, as people choose to sin. How much more evidence could we need, to know that God's will *isn't* done on earth as it is in heaven? The doctrine of absolute sovereignty says that God always gets what he wants, but passages like Genesis 6:5-6 and Hosea 11:1-2 and Ezekiel 33:11 and Luke 13:34 show the Lord not getting what he wants.

There is also a problem with premises 3 and 4, which contain the implicit supposition that we can tell who is saved by looking at them. Certainly, some people evidence their faith more strongly than others, but can we really dare to suppose that we know that

God is not at work in some of the people around us? Jesus commanded us "Do not judge." How then can we offer the judgment that because these people don't show the marks of salvation, they clearly are not among the saved?

Moreover, if we build a doctrine of who is saved and who is lost by looking around, that is not Calvinistic epistemology. The epistemology of Calvinism is an epistemology of revelation, which means that the proper means for Calvin and his followers to discover what to believe about the world of people around us is by gathering the biblical passages that speak to a given issue. Once we have done that, we remain fallible humans who must be humble in our reasoning, and who therefore need to turn back to the Bible once more, testing our reasoning against the witness of scripture.

When we do, we encounter many texts that speak of God's love for all the world, and indeed, of God's intention to save all the world. How did these texts affect Calvin's thinking? Here are his two relevant paragraphs of commentary on God's "not wishing that any should perish" in 2 Peter 3:9.

> *This is His wondrous love toward the human race, that He desires all men to be saved, and is prepared to bring even the perishing to safety. We must notice the order, that God is prepared to receive all men into repentance, so that none may perish. These words indicate the means of obtaining salvation, and whoever of us seeks salvation must learn to follow in this way.*
>
> *It could be asked here, if God does not want any to perish, why do so many in fact perish? My reply is that no mention is made here of the secret decree of God by which the wicked are doomed to their own ruin, but only of His lovingkindness as it is made known to us in the Gospel. There God stretches out His hand to all alike, but He only grasps those (in such a way as to lead to Himself) whom He has chosen before the foundation of the world.*[4]

Calvin's first paragraph does a fine job telling us about what the text says. Any Calvinist should find hearty agreement here, both in terms of method and content. The text in 2 Peter indicates that God doesn't wish for any to perish but for all to reach repentance, and in response Calvin's comments extol the wondrous love of God, who wants for all to be saved and for none to perish. This is proper Calvinism as to content: God's astonishing gracious love, to save the world. It is also proper Calvinism as to method: This is what the scripture teaches, so we are confident to believe it.

But the part that most people would "recognize" as Calvinistic is the second paragraph. That paragraph strays from Calvin's best thinking, both in its content and in its method.

Calvin's high doctrine of sovereignty might have led him to say, "The text says God wants everyone to be saved; sovereignty means that (at least by the end) God always gets what he wants; therefore all will at last reach salvation — glory be to God!"

That, however, is not what he said. Instead we have this second paragraph, where he asks, "If God does not want any to perish, why do so many in fact perish?" It appears to me that there are two problems here. First, his question assumes as a fact something that we are not in a position to say, because *we do not know* how many, in fact, perish, and (as noted above) our Lord forbids us to offer our judgment about whether any given individual is one of the perishing. Second, Calvin answers his question by pointing out that "no mention is made here of the secret decree of God by which the wicked are doomed to their own ruin." True enough. The text in 2 Peter 3 makes no mention of any secret decree of God that damns the wicked. Yet if there is no mention here of this secret decree, is it good exposition to teach it?

Calvin might well argue that other texts of scripture teach this secret decree, and insist that he is only expressing the idea here for the sake of balance and completeness. Yet, although Calvin was quite sure of this, it would be hard to point to a text that teaches "there is a secret decree of God by which the wicked are doomed." It was on the basis of his doctrine of sovereignty that Calvin worked his way to the idea that there must have been a secret decree of God, before the foundation of the world, whereby some were chosen for redemption and others for perdition. Calvin *reasoned* his way to this conclusion; he did not *read* it from the pages of the Bible.

Just because Calvin reasoned his way to that conclusion doesn't mean he was wrong. If indeed God decided to create some for salvation and some for damnation, that would have been established by some "secret decree" of God — secret because such things are forever beyond the ability of the human mind to fathom.

Yet, if Calvin had applied his own methodology at this point, he would have had to say, "Scripture does not teach about any secret decree of God whereby the wicked are doomed to their own ruin. So we who have set ourselves to learn of God from the scriptures have no basis for declaring that our Lord ever made any such decree." To say something along those lines would have been to follow his own advice, cited above:

> *Let this, therefore, be our sacred rule, not to seek to know anything about [predestination] except what Scripture teaches us. Where the Lord closes His holy mouth, let us also stop our minds from going on further.*[5]

Indeed, Calvin might well have hesitated even further, at this point, by saying something like this: "As a thoughtful Christian, I have read the scriptures and done my best to understand how God has gone about the business of saving the world. I have drawn together many texts and concluded that there must have been an eternal decree within the secret counsel of God, creating some for salvation and others for damnation. I have arrived at a well-worked-out doctrine. Yet, what will I do, when I come across texts like this one in 2 Peter and the many others that speak of God's love for all the world, God's desire to save all the world? Will I find a way to modify these passages, so that they reflect my doctrine? Or will I find a way to modify my doctrine, so that it reflects the truth of these texts?"

As it turns out, Calvin did not ask himself that question. Thus in his discussion of 2 Peter 3:9, as noted above, Calvin ended up offering comments to modify the meaning of the text, rather than reconsidering his doctrine. The biblical text Calvin was reading says that God wants everyone to reach redemption. But Calvin ended up teaching that these words that tell us God wants to save all the world need to be read in the light of God's secret decree that indicates God *doesn't* want to save all the world.

This failing is not peculiar to Calvin, of course. Whenever we have put in great effort to gain insight into some difficult problem, it is hard to hear evidence that counts against us. Most of us would not intuitively ask ourselves the kind of question that I have proposed that Calvin might have asked, "Will I find a way to modify these Bible passages so that they teach the same as my doctrine, or will I find a way to modify my doctrine so that it teaches the same as these texts?" To do so would require us to be substantially more self-critical than normal. Even so, if Calvin had managed to put himself on the spot that way, it seems clear to me that his response would have been straightforward. He would choose the witness of scripture over his best previous understanding, and the history of doctrine would have proceeded in quite a different fashion.

It didn't happen that way, however. Thus Calvin's stark doctrine of predestination became established, instead. Even then, although Calvin firmly believed it, predestination never was the key to his theology; grace and gratitude were the major themes of Calvin's own thinking. It was only in the thinking of succeeding generations that *Calvinism* and *predestination* became synonymous.

Interestingly enough, the two key New Testament texts that directly address this topic have a rather different way of talking about predestination.

> *Those whom God foreknew he also predestined to be conformed to the image of his Son, in order that he might be the first-born in a large family. And those whom he predestined he also called; and those whom he called he also justified; and those whom he justified he also glorified.* — Romans 8:29-30

> *God chose us in Christ before the foundation of the world to be holy and blameless before him in love. He predestined us for adoption as his children through Jesus Christ, according to the good pleasure of his will.* — Ephesians 1:4-5

The first thing to note here is that these texts talk about people being people predestined to redemption. They do not mention the idea of predestination to damnation.

Many people are quite surprised to discover this. They sometimes respond by supposing that if you talk about one, that implies some sort of tacit balancing statement that must be expressed by the reader. That is, having learned that some are predestined to heaven, the reader is expected to draw the conclusion — a necessary, inevitable conclusion — that others must have been predestined to hell.

There are three reasons for hesitating here, however.

First, Paul said one of these things; he didn't say the other. He said that God predestined people to life; he did not say that God predestined others to damnation. So it is possible to say that God has elected us to adoption, to justification, to glorification, without saying anything at all in the other direction. That's what Paul has actually done, in these texts of scripture. Whoever is damned, whatever the reason that they are damned, Paul has not said that it is because God predestined them to be damned.

Second, there is no reason to suppose that God's decisions regarding salvation must be balanced. If God allows all the world to go to hell as the just punishment for our sins, that would be God's right. If God chooses to redeem every individual who has ever lived, that would be God's right. If God decides to save some and damn others, that would be God's right. In any such case, God's action would be one of freedom, rather than being compelled by some external circumstance. God does not say, "Oh, wait, what about balance? The need for balance compels me to choose the balanced way of doing election." God acts in freedom. There is nothing outside of God — certainly not some arbitrary decision on our part as to what would count as balance — that requires God to act in any particular way.

Third, it is problematic whenever we place an inference we have drawn from scripture on the same level of authority as scripture's own words. Inferences are one of the chief means for building our understanding of scripture's message; they are a necessary part of the process of comprehension. But inferences are not the Bible. It's one thing to claim biblical authority for a verse I read in scripture — it's quite another to claim biblical authority for an idea that might be implied by that verse.

Suppose, then, that we read these two key biblical texts that speak about predestination, and note that they speak of predestination to redemption. God has chosen a destiny for us, before we could have chosen such a destiny for ourselves, indeed before the foundation of the earth: We are predestined for glory, we are predestined to live in holiness and love before God, we are predestined to be the very children of God.

A few moments ago we hesitated about supposing that if some are predestined to heaven, that must mean that others are predestined to damnation. Do the texts from Ephesians and Romans then leave us with the conclusion that everyone must be saved? After all, if these things are our destiny — indeed, if this is the destiny that God Almighty has chosen for us — doesn't that make this just as inevitable as the predestination to hell we were worried about before?

Exercise 7-1
1. Using a concordance, a topical study Bible, your own recollection, on-line resources, or any other study aids you like, make a list of half a dozen or so texts that speak to the sovereignty of God's will, passages that indicate, one way or another, that God always gets what he wants.

   _____
   _____
   _____
   _____

   Now make another list, of passages that indicate instances where God doesn't get what he wants.

   _____
   _____
   _____
   _____

Consider these two lists of texts. Consider the conclusion you might draw from each of them: God always gets what he wants; God doesn't always get what he wants. You might feel pretty uncomfortable, faced with these two contrasting lists of passages. Yet one of the conclusions probably seems to resonate more with you than the other, as it reflects more of your perception of how things really are.

2. Take the other point of view for a moment. Do your best to write three or four sentences of sympathetic exposition of the viewpoint you disagree with, explaining why (despite texts to the contrary) it really does make good sense to hold to that point of view.

_____
_____
_____
_____
_____

As you have seen in this exercise, there are texts that offer strong support for either viewpoint; a decent argument can be made either way. Most likely you will continue to be more persuaded in one direction that the other. Perhaps the best statement that can be made, as an overall summary, is this: "We (the Christian church overall, across denominations, perspectives, and history) *do not know* what is the best way to understand how the predestination of God turns out." Within your own understanding, you probably find one point of view more persuasive, and you can offer that as the perspective that you think (probably) makes most sense. When you do, you need to offer it humbly, in the recognition that we do not yet know how it all comes out.

Do you recall what happened when the Blue Fairy decided to give Pinocchio the opportunity to become a real boy? She set in motion a series of events that no one else in the story could possibly have imagined. What an astonishing idea — to take a marionette, hanging by its strings against the back wall of

Gepetto's studio, and choose for it the destiny of becoming a real boy.

Pinocchio began his adventures, and he did some things and said some things rather well. Still, we should acknowledge frankly that there were a number of things that he got quite wrong.

Many of the things he did well, and many of the things he got wrong, centered around the question of friendship. Pinocchio learned that your friends can provide strength and encouragement in time of need. He learned that your friends can lead you in the wrong direction, and get you in trouble. And he learned that with some friends, your heart will be broken when they are lost.

Perhaps the clearest observation we can make is that becoming a real boy is not easy. Even when you have been predestined to become a real boy, it is far from automatic. As the story progresses, there are times when it seems more than likely that Pinocchio's destiny will never be fulfilled.

Which would mean that the Blue Fairy would not get what she wants. She chose a destiny for Pinocchio, a destiny that he as a marionette could never have chosen for himself. She wants him to become a real boy, but it often appears that her intention will end up being frustrated.

When we are reading (or listening to, or watching) a story like Pinocchio, we cannot yet tell how it will come out. Certainly, Pinocchio cannot tell how it will come out. ("Ah," you say, "but I have heard the story before — I already know how it comes out." Perhaps so. Even then, if you know something from your privileged position *outside* the story, you need to see that Pinocchio does not know and cannot know, from his position *inside* the story. And — are you quite sure you know how this one comes out? You may remember how it ended last time you heard a story about a marionette destined to become a real boy; but possibly this one is a little different, perhaps this story does not end up happily ever after. Not every story does, you know.)

Perhaps even the Blue Fairy herself is not sure how it will end up. Indeed, there are points in the story where you might well suppose that the Blue Fairy should conclude that her experiment has become a failure. She may have chosen this grand destiny for

Pinocchio, but he isn't getting it. Perhaps the wisest course, then, is for her to turn him back into a marionette and set him once again in his place, hanging against the studio's back wall.

If she does this, he will not cause any more trouble. He will not experience any more heartbreak. He will not tell any more lies. And he will never become a real boy.

But it is his destiny to become a real boy. And the Blue Fairy really wants Pinocchio's destiny to be fulfilled. She wants him to become a real boy. She does not cancel the experiment. The story keeps on going and we keep listening, hoping to find out that Pinocchio does indeed fulfill his destiny, and become a real boy.

But wait a moment. Is it right to suggest that the Blue Fairy herself might not know whether her plan is going to work in the end? If the Blue Fairy has the power to choose a destiny for Pinocchio, doesn't that mean she would know whether he will fulfill that destiny? Or is the issue just as much in doubt for her as it is for him?

As to that, the best and bravest answer we can give is that we do not know.

We don't have access to the mind of the Blue Fairy. Perhaps she has a source of knowledge that we are not aware of that enables her genuinely to know the future. Then again, perhaps what she knows about the future is that the future is not yet real. It is full of possibilities which might become facts, but as of now they are not facts. Suppose she is completely aware of every single possibility. If she knows all that, then surely she knows the difference between something that is possible and something that is real. She would not mistake a possibility for a fact. She would be well aware that almost all of the possibilities will not become real. She would be clear that one of the possibilities is that Pinocchio could become a real boy. And another possibility is that he will fail to do so. But she would not know either of these as a fact, because neither of them is a fact — not yet.

Whatever you may think of that — whatever you may think of the foreknowledge even of Almighty God — it remains true that we do not know how the story comes out, when we are in the midst of it. We read testimony in the Bible that indicates that God has chosen for us a destiny of becoming real boys and girls — long before we could have imagined any such thing. God made a decision on our behalf — to take us from being like puppets, where other factors were continually pulling our strings and making us jump in odd directions, and to transform us that we might genuinely become the children of God. We also read testimony in the Bible of how some do not end up fulfilling this destiny: wide is the gate and broad the road that leads to destruction, and many follow it. When we look to the power of God's grace, it seems that God's will must be fulfilled. When we look to the perverseness that emerges so often in our own hearts, we recognize that there is room for uncertainty.

Will the will of God be fulfilled? Or will it be frustrated?

The best and bravest answer we can give is that we do not know.

We cannot know, because we are in this particular story. We are in the middle of the story; we are not at the end of it.

When we get to the end of the story, then we will know. There could be a lot of surprises, by the end of the story, and since God is the one who originally put this story together, there is much reason for hope.

After all, God's grace and my resistance are not balanced. God's grace is much deeper, much more persistent, much wiser than my perverseness. While I cannot claim to know how it will turn out, I have good reason to place much more confidence in God than in myself.

Besides, I think the princess' wisdom and beauty and laughter is going to get to the prince, in spite of all his churlishness.

Don't you have to wonder what's with that boy, anyway? That's what the courtiers said to each other. Why doesn't the prince get over that attitude? Why doesn't he see that acting like a jerk, just so you can prove that you have the freedom to be a jerk, isn't the most important thing in the world?

The prince asked himself that same question. "She is so much better than I deserve," he thought. "If I didn't have such a chip on my shoulder, I could fall in love with her in five minutes. And what if I refuse? I could keep on behaving as badly as I can, spurning this gift that has been offered to me — and I'd end up living out the rest of my days unhappily ever after."

Which will he choose?

Perhaps the storyteller can only shrug at this point and concede that the story hasn't yet gotten that far. When you are telling a true story, you can only tell the ending of the story when you know what the ending is. When you are living in the middle of a true story, you don't yet know how it will come out.

Putting this in terms of the doctrine of predestination, we believe God has destined us for glory. He has chosen to love us (grace), and invited us to respond by falling in love with him (gratitude). That's God's purpose. But in the end, will the purpose of Almighty God be fulfilled? Or will it be frustrated? Will God get what he wants? We are not in a position to say, because we don't have full knowledge of how the mind of God works, and because *we're in the middle of this story*. We can't know how it comes out, because we haven't yet gotten to the end. Perhaps we will accept this astonishing gift of God's love offered to us, clearly far better than we deserve. Or perhaps we will keep on behaving as badly as we can, spurning the gift that has been offered to us, and living out the rest of our days unhappily ever after.

Still, there's something about that princess.

Why is the princess so crazy about this guy? Whatever it is that moves her, she sounds both creative and determined in this irrepressible love that she offers. Love is not compulsion, but there was something about her love that was mighty compelling. Day by day, in her glances, in her smile, in the gestures of her hands, she invited him to reconsider whether he wanted to go on being so stubborn.

There came the day when the prince realized that the laughter in her voice was getting to him. He hadn't really made up his mind whether he was going to let himself fall in love or not, but it was happening, even so. He was in danger of being swept right off his feet. Did he want to be swept right off his feet? He wasn't sure. Maybe that would be a good thing. Still, even though he felt a little stodgy about it, he thought he had better give himself some time to ponder the implications of all this.

So he pondered. He thought, "It's up to me to decide. I said that I would only marry whomever I want, whenever I want. And that much has certainly become clear — it's up to me to make my own free choice, to marry her or not."

He sat in silence for another minute, realizing that he was just about convinced that what he wanted more than anything else in the world was to be in love with her forever.

Because you are interested in the doctrine of predestination, you probably already see something that the prince did not yet see (because he was, naturally enough, focusing on his own situation): When the prince gets around to deciding to marry the princess, he will have chosen freely; yet his decision will come as no surprise to the princess, for she has known all along that it is his destiny to love her as fully as she loves him.

The princess was sitting on a marble bench in the garden, enjoying the afternoon sunshine and reading her book, when the prince walked up to her. For a moment she pretended that she was so engrossed in her book that she had not seen him. Then she looked up at him and smiled.

"I've been acting like a jerk," he said.

"Yes," she said, "you have." There was no recrimination in her voice, just acknowledgment.

"I've been so stubborn about wanting to make my own choice."

"Yes," she said again, with the corners of her eyes crinkling in that delightful way, "you have."

And the prince looked at her, really looked at her, as if he had never looked at her before. He said, "It took me a while to figure it out. I hope I can do better from now on. I intend to. If you'll still have me. Because what I finally realized is, I have fallen in love with you."

And with a laugh of full of gladness and grace she said, "Yes. You have."

And she stood up, put her arms around his neck, and kissed him. It was a powerful kiss, a kiss of passion and purity and promise. Indeed, in all the history of kissing, this was the second-best kiss there ever has been. The annals and archives of the kingdom keep close records on this sort of thing, and it is quite clear — only one kiss has ever surpassed it.

That was the kiss at their wedding.

And they lived happily ever after.

Exercise 7-2

As we have seen, various aspects of the doctrine of predestination might be explored by telling a story about a prince and princess, about a park ranger rescuing teenagers, or about Pinocchio and the Blue Fairy. Here are two more story starters.

1. Monica had always been a worrier. She was more of a worrier than most any other fourth grader in her class. This evening, though, she was particularly worried. She had been thinking about God, and thinking about God is frequently worrisome, whether you are in the fourth grade, or are old, like in college, or ancient, like thirty. Monica was worried because it had occurred to her that God was in charge of the world. Some people might suppose, from the state of the world, that God wasn't doing too good a job with being in charge of things. But that's not the direction that Monica's thoughts had taken. Instead, she was thinking about heaven and hell. If God was in charge of everything, then God was in charge of heaven and hell. Monica believed in Jesus, and she hoped she believed in him well enough that God would want her in heaven; but she wasn't sure. If God was in charge, she figured, that meant it was up to God to decide, and what if God had decided that she wasn't one of the people he wanted in heaven?
2. Amos woke up feeling grubby. For the last four nights he had been sleeping in an alley, but yesterday evening there had been too much noise in the neighborhood and he hadn't gotten much rest. He hadn't had a bath in a week and a half. His mouth felt gritty, he was hungry, and he was far from home. Home! He thought about his home, he could

almost see the family farm, with the grain standing tall, looking so fine, promising a wonderful harvest. Then he saw a pair of grasshoppers, gently held in the hand of God, and in a moment the two grasshoppers had become fifty grasshoppers, then thousands, and then millions of them, and they ate up all the grain. They ate every green leaf in sight, and left nothing but dust in the fields. Amos said, "O God! Don't do this! Forgive the sins of your people, for they are too few to survive this calamity!" And God shrugged and said, "This is the punishment I have chosen for them, so this is what will happen. Do you think I the Lord God will change my mind, just because you ask me to?"

Choose one of these story starters (or another of your own creation). Fill it out with some further details — relatives and friends, questions and unsatisfying answers, actions and conflicts. Use that story as the framework for a sermon that will enable your congregation to get more of a handle on the doctrine of predestination.

Predestination is not, of course, everyone's favorite doctrine. It may be that it is a topic on which you would never have chosen to preach (though perhaps I have intrigued you enough to change that). At the least, I hope that I have motivated you to consider using narrative as a tool that makes it possible to preach sermons that address doctrine. Another example, preaching on the doctrine of death and eternal life, is in the next chapter.

---

1. B. A. Gerrish, *Grace and Gratitude: the Eucharistic Theology of John Calvin* (Minneapolis: Augsburg Fortress, 1993).

2. David W. Torrance and Thomas F. Torrance, eds., *Calvin's New Testament Commentaries*, vol. 8, E. T. R. MacKenzie (Grand Rapids, Michigan: William B. Eerdmans, 1960), pp. 202-203.

3. Among many fine treatments of this issue, Mark Twain's *The Mysterious Stranger* offers an especially powerful narrative exploration of the problem of sovereignty.

4. *Op cit*, David W. Torrance and Thomas F. Torrance, eds., pp. 364-365.

5. *Ibid*, p. 203.

Chapter 8

If Only You Had Been Here

*preaching the doctrine of death
and eternal life as a story*

Lillian came to live at Neville Manor nursing home in Cambridge, Massachusetts, in the winter of 1981. I was a student chaplain there at the time, in my middle year of seminary, and Lillian was assigned a room in the wing where I visited; and that's how I met her. Dear Jesus, what would my life have been like if I had never met her?

Lillian had been struck by polio when she was a teenager. For the next 43 years she had lived at home, with her mother, and the two of them did pretty well as a family, taking care of each other. But the disease had grown progressively more crippling. Over the years, her mother's health had become quite frail as well. The time came when she could no longer take care of Lillian; it was all she could do just to take care of herself; and Lillian came to Neville Manor.

I visited with Lillian from week to week. We told stories. We laughed at each other's jokes.

She told me about how one time her mother had opened the refrigerator on Easter Sunday morning, and there was the Easter bunny. Her mother was quite surprised by this, and said, "What are you doing in my refrigerator?"

The Easter bunny said, "This *is* a Westinghouse, isn't it?"

Lillian's mother said, "Errr, yes, it is, but...."

The Easter Bunny kind of shrugged, and said, "So I'm westing."

I told Lillian about how one of the deacons had come up to me after Sunday school the previous week, with a troubled look on his face. He was supposed to do a children's lesson, and he didn't know where to look to find the original story about Easter eggs in the Bible, and could I help him find it?

Lillian got this impish look on her face, and she said, "I hope you told him to look just before the part about the Pilgrims and the first Thanksgiving."

So we laughed together. We agreed that Easter wasn't just bunnies and eggs. We talked about some of the Bible stories you actually can find in the Bible. We prayed for each other. She seemed like such a cheery individual. I liked her a lot.

Only later did I find out how bleak she had felt, when she first came to Neville Manor. She had thought she and her mother had done well, they'd worked together as a good team, a strong team, for many years. Now that was over. In her despair she didn't know how to go on. She told me I had saved her life, during that desolate time when she didn't know what to do, and so she decided to give me a gift.

I graduated from seminary, became an ordained minister, and moved to Kansas to serve my first parish. I wrote to her from time to time — not as often as I should have. We went back to Boston on vacation one time, and I stopped by to visit her. A few years later, we moved back to Massachusetts. Every once in a while I would drive in to Cambridge to see her. I wish I had gone more often.

During all this time, when I was doing a good job of keeping in touch and when I was not, she gave me her gift. Throughout these ten years she prayed for me, and for my family, and for my ministry, every single day, until she died in 1992. That was the gift she had decided to give.

It was near Christmas in 1990 that she told me the story of her early years with polio. By then she was entirely bedfast, with her right arm all shriveled and twisted, and just a little mobility remaining in her left arm.

The disease struck in the fall of 1938, when she was fifteen, a high school sophomore. Lillian was not severely crippled in her early years with polio, but badly enough to make her give up two of the great loves of her life. The first to go was ice skating. Ever since she was a young girl, Lillian loved to skate. After she got polio she could still get around pretty well on crutches, for quite a number of years; but she could never ice skate again.

The other great love that polio made her give up was a boy named John. They were high school sweethearts, from early in freshman year, all the way to graduation. Lillian told me about the senior prom. She had never taken dance lessons, and she had lost the gracefulness she had once had as a skater. She had not wanted to go to the prom at all, because she was embarrassed about how awkward she would look, standing there on crutches in the middle of the dance floor. But John had persuaded her, and he held her in his arms and slowly, slowly turned with her in time to the music, and Lillian felt as if she were floating, in the wonder of that magic evening.

Then, after she and John graduated from Cambridge High School, in June of 1941, Lillian told John good-bye. She told me it was the second bravest thing she ever did. John told her he loved her, he didn't care if she had polio. Yes, he knew it would give them challenges, but he wanted to marry her anyway. "No," she said. "You will find someone who can be the wife that you deserve, who can be a mother to your children like they will deserve." And Lillian told him good-bye.

I said, "Wow."

I said, "If that is only the second bravest thing you ever did, you already have more courage than about anyone I have ever met."

She lay there in silence for a moment. I stood next to her bed. Neither of us spoke. The silence was not uncomfortable.

The eleventh chapter of the gospel of John tells part of the story of a family — a brother and two sisters, Lazarus, Mary, and Martha. They lived in a small village outside Jerusalem, and they were close friends with Jesus. Lazarus got very sick. They sent for Jesus — Jesus the healer, Jesus the miracle worker. "When Jesus gets here, everything will be all right," they said. But Jesus didn't get there. Mary and Martha prayed that Jesus would hurry, but Jesus didn't hurry. Then Lazarus died. Finally, four days later, Jesus arrived.

When Martha saw Jesus, she said, "Lord, if only you had been here, my brother would not have died." Then a few minutes later, when Mary saw Jesus, she said, "Lord, if only you had been here, my brother would not have died." Probably this was a cry of grief, more than a cry of accusation. It may sound like anger or reproach when someone says something like this to you; it can sound like they're blaming it on you. The best move is to not take it personally. Take it as grief rather than blame.

In their grief, Martha and Mary cried out, "Lord, if only you had been here, my brother would not have died." But, of course, he would have — people do. Some die sooner, and some die later. We're scarcely ever ready. Perhaps Lazarus would have died ten years later, or forty years later, but he would have died.

"Jesus, if only you had been here, my brother would not have died," they said. But Jesus has been there, time after time, when beloved brothers and sisters have died. Jesus has been there, time after time, across twenty centuries of time, as Christians have died. Isn't it tempting to suppose that if only Jesus had been here, my wife, my husband, my parent, my child, would not have died? But Jesus was here, every time. Jesus has been present, all along the way. And still all those beloved people went ahead and died.

Mary and Martha and Jesus went to the grave. Jesus wept, it says in John 11:35. That's all that verse says.

(You know, preacher, Christians ought to memorize more Bible verses. Probably there are quite a few of the people in your congregation who have learned John 3:16, the best-known verse of all. If that's the only Bible verse they have ever memorized, you can double their inventory if you can get them to learn John 11:35 as well. Just two words: Jesus wept.)

Why did Jesus weep? In just a moment Jesus will call out, "Lazarus, come forth," and Lazarus will come forth. Jesus stands at the tomb of Lazarus, and weeps. Why does he weep, two minutes before he calls Lazarus forth from the dead? I know why Mary says, "Lord, if you had been here, my brother would not have died," and then weeps at her brother's grave. I know why Martha says, "Lord, if you had been here, my brother would not have died," and then weeps at her brother's grave. But why does Jesus weep? Jesus the king of the ages, Christ the eternal Son of God, Jesus the Lord of life, who became human for this very purpose — to die for our sins, to be raised for our life — why does he weep at the tomb of

Lazarus? He is about to shout, "Lazarus come forth," in the knowledge that at his word Lazarus will indeed come forth. Why then does Jesus weep?

Once upon a time, there was a children's book that told a wonderful and powerful story, a story so fine, a story of love and honor, hope and glory. As it turns out, even the introduction to this story was quite fascinating. And here is what happened. A mother began to read this book to her children, starting with the first page of the introduction. The children loved it. Indeed, the children fell completely in love with the introduction. The children loved the introduction so much that when their mother came to the end of the introduction, the children said, "Please, please, read the introduction again! Let's not ever turn the page to the rest of the story. Read the introduction — read it again and again so that it never ends."

Once upon a time, there was a musical. It was filled with stirring passionate songs, and it had a tenor solo so lovely that it made the angels weep for joy. Like many musicals, it began with an overture. It was an especially fine overture, incorporating snippets of those stirring passionate songs, and introducing the theme of that tenor solo. The audience gathered for the musical, and the orchestra played the overture. The audience fell in love with the overture. Oh, how they clapped and cheered! They shouted out loud, "Encore! Encore! Play the overture again. Play the overture so that it lasts forever and let's not ever segue to the show itself!"

Once upon a time, there was a high school. It was full of lively students who were great friends. They studied together and played sports and went on outings and did service projects. They talked about religion and faithfulness and the meaning of life. They wondered about the future — college and marriage and careers and children. They were thoughtful and observant teens, and they saw something that had happened for many people who were no longer teenagers. They saw the way that so many friendships established in high school fade away with the passing of time. It may sound strange to say they had fallen in love with high school, but perhaps that is not too strong a term, for as graduation grew near they said, "Oh! Let's just go on like this forever. Let's go on sharing in laughter and friendship. Let these high school days never end, so that we never have to lose the closeness and camaraderie we have right now."

I remember standing there in Neville Manor, at Lillian's bedside, for several minutes in silence, holding her hand. I have stood by bedsides before and since, where nobody had any words to say, and that silence can sometimes feel quite awkward; but this silence was somehow full of assurance. Part of my soul was simply glad to hold her hand, smile at her, and nod a little. Part of my soul was somehow back in 1941, admiring the resolute decision of that young woman who wanted the best for her true love and, for the second-bravest decision she ever made, sent him off to find a wife.

After a while I said, "If you would care to tell me the bravest thing, I would be very glad to listen."

After another moment she nodded, and said, "All right." And then she told me how that had come about.

It was in December of 1945, after John came home from World War II. By then Lillian sometimes still got out on crutches, but mostly she was at home in a wheelchair. John came to her house, and asked her again to marry him. He had seen the frailty of life, as the army fought its way across France. He had been sure he was going to die in the Battle of the Bulge. All he had wanted, as the German shells were falling all around, was to make it home. Home to her. And here he was. Home with her. Would she marry him?

Again she told him, "No." She cried as she told him. She cried as she told me, 45 years later. I cried, too. "No," Lillian told him. "You will find someone. There is a woman out there, somewhere, a woman who is sound in body, a woman who can be a wife the way you deserve, a woman who can give you a family. You will find that someone, and you will fall in love. You'll see."

"I only want you," said John.

"No," said Lillian. And then, again, she told him good-bye.

And John did find someone — Mary Catherine. Lillian said she wished she had had the courage to go to their wedding, but she wasn't brave enough for that. She did find the courage to go to their church a year later, and again a year after that, to see the baptisms of their first two children. Shortly after that, John and

Mary Catherine and the two little ones moved across the country to Oregon, and Lillian lost track of them. But, she had seen them at those two baptisms. She saw those two beautiful babies. She saw the adoration in Mary Catherine's eyes. She had never seen a more handsome man, had never seen a more manly man than John, as he stood there beside Mary Catherine at those two baptisms. Lillian cried at those two baptisms. But she also smiled.

The message of Christ's resurrection is available all year long, but on Easter Sunday we pay particular attention to what this thing is supposed to mean. It is because of the resurrection that we can believe the message that Jesus died for the sins of the world. It is because of the resurrection that we can believe that death is not the end of the story. It is because of the resurrection that we can believe the gospel, and thereby know that in life and in death we belong to the Lord, and that we will forever be with the Lord.

The message of Christ's resurrection is available all year long, but on Easter Sunday there will also be more people present to explore and ponder and celebrate the resurrection than on any other day of the year.

This bothers many preachers. Perhaps you are one of them, feeling troubled as you look at all the people who have showed up for Easter, and think about how those people will not be back again until Christmas. Many preachers get upset about this, when they think about these people, many of them officially church members in good standing. What is wrong with these people, that they think it sufficient for their Christian life to attend worship twice a year?

Yet those usually absent faces within the Easter crowd are not to be despised, but beloved. Many of them are wondering if the church has a message of hope to share in the face of death. Can the resurrection of Jesus make a difference for them, in their bereavement? They know the story says Jesus was raised from the dead long ago. But the person they loved who died this year was not raised from the dead. Does the church have a message of hope to offer them?

Many of these occasional attenders are rather jaded, because they have been burned before. How many times have they been present at funerals, with hearts aching for a word of comfort, and have found only condemnation? Does the church have a message of hope to offer them? Apparently not. Why bother, then, to come and listen to another reprimand, another judgment, another scolding for failing to be devout or righteous or dedicated enough?

Yet, on Easter here they are, somehow willing to try once again, hoping that perhaps this year there will come a word that touches the place in their heart that still aches with grief, touches it with the comfort of God.

This isn't the issue for all of them, of course. Not everyone who is present on Easter Sunday is in mourning. There are worshipers who are not at the moment seeking the meaning of death, but the meaning of life; the question of how the resurrection of Jesus moves people out and forward to change the world is addressed in chapter 9. In this chapter, though, we will note that among those present on Easter morning are those who really do long to find hope in the face of death.

Many an Easter sermon has been constructed to prove the historicity of the resurrection to these seekers and doubters. The motivation behind this is worthy; it stems from the conviction, "If these people ever just fully understood that Jesus is raised from the dead, it would change their lives."

It should be noted, though, that the four gospel writers evidence very little concern to prove the resurrection to their readers. They all testify to the resurrection, in powerful and evocative ways, but they certainly don't make much effort to provide answers to obvious questions people might raise. Any faithful reader of the four gospels knows there are many passages that demonstrate nearly word-for-word parallelism; it is not always clear which writer incorporated the text of his predecessor, but some sort of literary dependence appears to be pretty well established. In contrast to this, the stories the four evangelists tell of the empty tomb and the risen Jesus vary considerably from one another, with no discernible effort to make sure their accounts line up.

Exercise 8-1

Back in chapter 2, the third exercise looks at the contrasts in the death and resurrection narratives in a big picture way. This exercise invites you to notice some of the specific details that form those contrasts. Begin by reading the resurrection texts from the four gospels: Matthew 28:1-20; Mark 16:1-8; Luke 24:1-53; John 20:1—21:25.

1. How many women go to the tomb? What are their names?
   Matthew: _____
   Mark: _____
   Luke: _____
   John: _____

2. What do they expect? What do they find?
   Matthew: _____
   Mark: _____
   Luke: _____
   John: _____

3. What does Jesus say, at the tomb? To whom does he say it?
   Matthew: _____
   Mark: _____
   Luke: _____
   John: _____

4. What incidents are mentioned in only one or two gospels?
   Matthew: _____
   Mark: _____
   Luke: _____
   John: _____

5. What time period is covered, from the beginning to the end of the Easter narrative?
   Matthew: _____
   Mark: _____
   Luke: _____
   John: _____

Instead of a careful uniformity of testimony, it is clear that the gospel writers include and highlight rather different testimonies. The story of Thomas and his doubts, or the account of the restoration of Peter — these are not to be found in any gospel except John. The story of the walk to Emmaus is neglected by every writer but Luke. There is something commission-like in each of the gospels, yet only in Matthew do we find the words of the Great Commission. Mark's account is very brief, and breaks off in an unexpected place.

You do see what this means, preacher, don't you? The four evangelists do not worry about "proving" the resurrection to us; instead, they tell particular stories in the hope that when we hear those stories, we will experience the presence of the risen Jesus, speaking to us.

Only John tells the story of Lazarus, Mary, and Martha — a resurrection story that is about the resurrection of someone other than Jesus, which nevertheless provides a substantial amount of teaching for us about the meaning of Jesus' own resurrection, and about what it does for us. Only in John do we read the words Jesus said when he was talking to Martha about the resurrection and the life. "If you believe in me," he told her, "though you die, even so you will live; whoever lives and believes in me will never die." It is an odd thing to say, isn't it? All down the centuries, Christians have lived in Jesus and believed in Jesus, and they have died. It is not the case that some of them have died. It is not the case that most of them have died. No. It's all of them. Was there, then, never one faithful Christian in all those generations?

Or were there faithful Christians, but Jesus was mistaken when he said they'd never die?

I believe there were faithful Christians, and I believe that Jesus was not mistaken. What that means is, in Jesus' conversation with Martha he changes the meaning of death, in those two successive sentences. It is not simply that he uses the term to mean one thing in the first clause and to mean something different, in the following one. Rather, he is indicating that the reality of death itself is getting changed. There will still be this biological moment where the heart stops and the brain waves cease, but from now on that corporeal cessation will not be the last word we can say. Because Jesus is the resurrection and the life, death is no longer the end of the story. It is not the point of the story, not even the main theme of the story. Because Jesus is the resurrection and the life, death is only an incident in the story.

Yet it is a powerful incident, an intensely emotional incident. When we Christians face death — even though we are facing death in the name of Jesus, the resurrection and the life — we feel strong feelings. Some of what we feel is fear. We've never been on the far side of this transition before, and that kind of situation generally does make people nervous. Yet I don't think most of what we feel is fear. We believe that Jesus was right when he declared, "I am the resurrection and the life." We believe we will be alive with him forevermore, so we don't need to be afraid. Yet we still feel strong emotion.

Why is that? It's because we have fallen in love with this earthly life. When God set us here in the place where we are, he surrounded us with so many fine things, and put us together with so many fine people. We have fallen in love with them. This part that we have fallen in love with is just the beginning, but we have fallen in love with the beginning, and it is hard to turn the page from the introduction to the rest of the story, it is hard to leave the overture for the rest of the show, it is hard to say farewell to high school days and move on to the rest of life.

Why does Jesus weep at the grave? Because he understands this. He weeps with Mary and Martha and with all who have ever lost a loved one. He understands how we've fallen in love and wish it could all keep going without this transition.

More than that, I think that Jesus, in his genuine humanness, *feels* it right then. He, himself, feels the tearing sense of loss at the death of Lazarus. He knows what it is to have fallen in love with this earthly life God has given to us.

There are some things that you cannot really understand except by experiencing them. You can study up on them; you can master the theory of how they work; but there is a quality to what these things are that can only genuinely be understood by experiencing them.

You can read books and listen to explanations about diving technique; you can watch people dive from the high board with skill and grace; but, you only fully know the existential reality of what it is all about if you yourself climb the ladder and go out to the end of the board, and look down at that water impossibly far below you.

You can read books and listen to explanations about marriage; you can watch people getting married, perhaps even from the role of bridesmaid or groomsman; but, only fully know the existential reality of what it is all about if you yourself stand in front of God and everyone, devoting yourself with the best promises you can make.

You can read books and listen to explanations about combat; you can sympathize with a friend who is suffering from post-combat stress; but you only fully know the existential reality of what it is all about if you yourself experience an enemy shooting at you on the field of battle.

We would want to say that the Omniscient One certainly understands the theory of how humans face heartbreaking grief when someone greatly beloved dies. And yet there is this difference between knowing this as knowledge and knowing it as experience, and in these moments when he himself experiences it as he stands before the grave of Lazarus, Jesus knows grief in a way that is qualitatively different from the way he understood this as a concept across eternity before his incarnation.

Jesus, God the Eternal Son, who came to earth to lay down his life for the forgiveness of all our sins and to be raised for the establishment of all our lives in God, knows best of all that this earthly life is simply prologue to the fullness of joy that we shall know in the wonder of eternal life. Even though he knows that, like us he has fallen in love with this life, and like us he weeps with grief to see it end.

Exercise 8-2

Select one of the less-well-known women who went to the tomb of Jesus, from one of the passages you examined in the last exercise. Do some exegetical reading, in commentaries and Bible reference materials, to discover as much of the back story for this woman as you can. Consider what you know and can guess, and then tell this woman's story. Let us see her personal sense of loss, in the death of a leader who has changed her life, her sense of duty that sends her to do the embalming, and her recognition that she can successfully go through the motions to do the things that need to be done, while feeling this terrible void that it seems nothing could ever fill again. Fill in some of the other details as you go, but do go ahead, and tell her story, and let us feel her grief.

After weeping at the grave of Lazarus, Jesus lifted up his voice and called out loud, "Lazarus, come forth!" And the dead man came forth out of the grave. When Lillian died, my soul cried out the same way, "Come forth, come back to life! Come and be my friend who prays for me, day by day. I miss you so much, I need you." But unlike Lazarus, she did not come back to life. Her corpse remained unmoving in her coffin, and then was lowered into the ground. Jesus established the promise of eternal life in his own resurrection. He demonstrated the promise of victory over death when he raised Lazarus. But when Lillian's corpse was lowered into the ground, that's where it stayed.

Yet, those promises are real, and they are in fact fulfilled. Lillian had turned the page from the introduction to the rest of her story; the overture had segued into the heart of the musical; she had graduated from prep school and moved into real life. For those who believe in Jesus, even though they die, nevertheless they live; indeed, those who live and believe in Jesus will never die.

The last time I saw Lillian, not long before she died, I told her, "Some day, Lillian, you're going to die and go to heaven, and then you won't have polio any more."

She said, "I'm looking forward to that."

"You were a pretty good ice skater, back in the day, I guess."

She smiled at the memory. "Yes. I had a lot of fun with it."

I said, "Lillian, after you die and go to heaven and don't have polio any more, and after I die and go to heaven, can I come by some time and we could go ice skating?"

She nodded. "I'd like that."

I said, "I'm kind of shaky as an ice skater. You'll have to go easy on me."

She laughed and she said, "No way. If you're going to skate with me, you have to skate like you really mean it. Don't worry. I'll teach you how."

Because this life God has given us is so good, we fall in love with it, big time, and even though we know it's only the beginning, we weep when it ends. I know I felt the assurance of God's love, stronger even that death, at Lillian's funeral; but I also know I cried, with such a strong sense of loss.

But because Jesus is the resurrection and the life, death doesn't get the final say. Because Jesus is the resurrection and the life, there's more of the story to come. Because Jesus is the resurrection and the life, later on in my story there's going to be this chapter about how Lillian teaches me to ice skate like I really mean it.

I'm looking forward to that.

Exercise 8-3

1. Consider these three passages.

    a. 1 Thessalonians 4:13-18 — This passage is intended to comfort people who are bereaved (4:18). It is a text people sometimes turn to when they want to put their hand to the vain exercise of guessing a timetable for

the second coming, but such speculations will only distract us from the intent of the passage: that we not grieve as others do who have no hope. This is not a statement that we do not grieve. Indeed we do grieve, yet our grief is not hopeless grief, but grief undergirded with hope.
- b. 1 Corinthians 15:50-58 — Throughout chapter 15, Paul reiterates the teaching that faith in the resurrection of Jesus is not in vain. In the end, flesh and blood does not inherit the kingdom, and so we shall not all sleep, but we shall all be changed, and death will be swallowed up in victory. ("We shall not all sleep, but we shall all be changed" does make an excellent poster for the wall of the church nursery, by the way.)
- c. John 20:24-29 — This is the third incident John gives us to reveal the character of Thomas the realist. (In John 11:7-8, 16, Thomas offers the clear-eyed assessment that following Jesus to Judea will mean death for his followers as well. In John 14:5 Thomas offers the frank admission that he does not know where Jesus is going.) Here he admits to his own inability to believe unless he sees for himself, and gets chided by Jesus: "Blessed are those who have not seen, and yet believed." Future generations of Christians will not have his experience, and yet they will come to believe with great assurance in the resurrection.

2. Consider as well a story of death and grief. This might find its source in a funeral you have done, or one you have attended, in the death of a beloved teenager or a beloved grandparent. Put together the pieces of this story: Who is the person who died? What are the incidents that shaped their life? Who are the people who were important to them? Who is it that is grieving?
3. Tell this story, interweaving insights from the passage you have chosen.

Chapter 9

I Am Sending You[1]

preaching the doctrine of resurrection and mission as a story

Long, long ago, in a universe far, far away, there was an adventure. A quest. A decision was made, a goal was set — a high and lofty goal, fraught with danger, yet offering such a wondrous reward.

It was a quest to rescue the people who lived in a distant kingdom. This kingdom had many names. It was sometimes called the Land of the Shadow of Death. That was because Death had captured the kingdom, had taken it over, had declared that he, Death, was the real king of that land. He wasn't, of course, and the people knew that, but his shadow seemed to stretch everywhere across the land, touching everything, nibbling at the edges of everyone's lives. You could never quite ignore the shadow of death. They knew, like a distant memory buried deep in their souls, sometimes nearly forgotten yet still there, that they were not created for death; they were created for life. Still the shadow of death hung over their land and over their lives, and no one could escape from its sadness and despair. And sooner or later Death himself would come personally for each individual, and there was no escape from him, either.

In the wisdom of the great king — the king of the universe and the true king of the kingdom that was now called the Land of the Shadow of Death — in the wisdom of the great king, a hero was chosen, to fulfill this quest, for the sake of the people of the land. This hero would have companions at certain points during the adventure, but there would also be moments when the hero would have to stand and do battle alone.

And it came to pass that the great king sent his son into the kingdom. He sent him secretly; by the great king's great power, he had him born as a baby. There was risk in this, for while he was a baby he would have no knowledge that he was actually the son of the great king. Even as a child he would only have a few clues. What if he misunderstood his mission? But the child grew strong and wise and brave. He read the ancient books, which told of the love of the great king for the people of the land and which told that one day the great king would send an anointed one, a messiah, to tell the people of his love and to set them free from the power of death. And sometimes the boy would climb up on top of the hill at the edge of town, and he would listen for the voice of the great king.

The boy's name was Salvation. That was the name they gave him when he was born. In the language the people of his village spoke, it was Yeshua. It was not an uncommon name, in that time and place, but sometimes he wondered whether it might mean something more in his case. Although we usually don't take much notice of it, people's names often do mean something. A boy could be named Frank, which means forthright or plain-spoken. He might go months or years never thinking about that, but from time to time he'll wonder if that name might tell him something about who he is. A girl could be named Grace, which sometimes means elegance of movement and sometimes means God's gift of forgiveness. She might go months or years never thinking about that, but from time to time she'll wonder if that name might tell her something about who she is. This boy, the boy whose name was Salvation, he, too, went long periods of time without ever thinking about his name. Yet, from time to time, he wondered if that name might tell him something about who he was.

He thought he had actually started to hear, sometimes, the whisper of the great king, "You are my son. I have sent you for a purpose." That would be a wondrous thing, the boy thought to himself. But then he would pause, and ask himself, "What if you're mistaken about all this? What if you've never really heard the voice at all? What if you go marching off to look for the purpose of the great king and accomplish nothing? Perhaps it's better," he told himself, "just to stick to my woodworking, to do my job, to mind my own business. Son of the great king! What a fantasy. Here we are in the Land of the Shadow of Death, and you'd better do your job and earn your living, because the end of your living comes all too soon."

If that had been the final thought the young man ever had on the subject, there would be no story to tell. But he continued to listen for the voice of the great king, and the conviction grew within him that the words he had heard were true. And he began to preach, and people listened, and a small band of followers gathered around the man whose name was Salvation, for they believed in him.

He taught them that, although they lived in the Land of the Shadow of Death, the great king was the true king of the land, and that he had a purpose for them. He taught them about how to live with one another. He taught them about himself. "I am the Messiah," he told them, "I am the one who the people have believed would some day come to set everyone free. I am the Light of the World," he told them. "I am the one who gives light and understanding and freedom to those who walk in shadow and darkness. I am the Bread of Life," he told them, "I am the one who comes to nourish your souls. I am the Good Shepherd, and I have come to lay down my life for all the lost sheep of this lost land. I am teacher and Lord, and I give you an example of how to love one another. I am the True Vine, and like branches in the vine you find your life and sustenance flowing from me. How can I say all these things? Because, before Abraham was, I Am; I Am the I Am. I am the Son of the Great King, and I am here to set you free."

Ah, how they loved him then. They wanted to hear every word; they wanted to follow him always, to be faithful and loyal no matter what. But Death was angry. And Death reached out an angry claw to strike him down. His companions tried to be brave, but their courage melted away as Death drew near, and they ran. Only the man whose name was Salvation was left, face-to-face with Death.

And Death laughed. Death laughed as the man whose name was Salvation was dragged through the mockery of a trial, as his head was crowned with a crown made not of gold but of thorns, sharp and cruel, with blood running down into his eyes. Death laughed as the man's arms were nailed into a wooden beam, "Take that, carpenter!" Death laughed as the man prayed, "Forgive them, for they don't know what they are doing," because even if they didn't know, Death knew. Death knew, and Death laughed. "So your name is Salvation?" Death mocked. "And you're the son of the great king? But this is my land, the Land of the Shadow of Death. I am the king here. And you're dead." Death laughed, as he reached in and ripped the soul free from the bloody body, leaving it lifeless, cold, dead.

Then there was silence. The day turned dark. Night fell. The sun came up the next day and went down again at night. Nothing had changed in the Land of the Shadow of Death. Some of the man's followers had crept back together, but there was nothing they could think of to do, nothing they could say. Death was still the king, and Death would always have the last word. So they sat and watched the shadows grow darker and felt the chains of fear wrapping around their hearts, tighter, heavier. And in the midst of the silence, all they could hear was the sound of soft laughing.

The laughter began to grow louder. It grew in intensity, too. There was something in how it sounded that they could not quite recognize, and they did not know what it could mean. It was different from all the laughter they had ever heard before; it was ringing laughter, ringing with joy, shining joy and exultant gladness. Along with the laughter they could hear the sound of a thousand bright trumpets and the singing of legions of angels. And suddenly there he was, the man whose name is Salvation, right in front of them. They had locked the doors, even though a locked door would not protect them against death, but they had locked the doors because people gripped with fear do desperate things. But locked door or not, there he was, the Son of the Great King, standing right in their midst, filled with laughter and victory and peace and glory. He laughed, a laugh that sparkled with such purity, such wonder, such splendor, a laugh filled with goodness and love. In that moment they felt the cold chains around their hearts fall away as their fear melted and their despair turned to wonder. And they laughed, too.

Then he explained to them that the power of death had now been broken and that the land would no longer be known as the Land of the Shadow of Death; now it would be called the Kingdom of God. They had thought their hearts were as full of joy as anyone's heart could ever be, but when he said that, when he said that the new name of the land would be the Kingdom of God, it seemed so wondrous that they could hardly bear it.

Then he explained to them about the plan of the Great King. He explained to them how a hero had been chosen. He looked into each one of their faces with a searching intensity, and he said to all of them and to each of them — and because he is the Son of the Great King, he could even look down the long stretches of time to see you and me, and to say it to all of us and to each of us — he said, "You are the hero that I have chosen. As the Father has sent me, so I am sending you. You are the hero, chosen according to the plan of the Great King, and your quest is to tell the people this great news. For even though Death's power has been broken, he will still lie to people and tell them that he rules. From now on, those who die will simply leave this land and come to live with me, but Death will lie and will tell people to be afraid, and he will tell them that he is the final answer and the only real power. But you (that's right, you — across the centuries he looked, from then until now, the man whose name means salvation looked, and he saw you, face-to-face), you are the hero I have chosen. You will make the difference for them, because in spite of your questions and in spite of your fears, you will show them and tell them that the message is true, that death has been defeated. As the Father has sent me, so I am sending you."

And we, the friends and followers of Jesus, the one whose name is Salvation, we can scarcely take it in. This may be a great and noble task we have been given, worthy of our greatest efforts, but we hardly feel worthy of such honor. We hardly feel capable of such responsibility. Perhaps he should send someone else.

Somehow the voice of our hesitation must have carried back along the corridors of time, for the Son of the Great King responded to our uncertainty. "On your quest," he said, "on your adventure, you will have companions who will help you and encourage you. There will be moments, however, when you will look around and see no one, and you will have to choose to stand for the truth even if you have to stand alone. Yet, because you are the hero I have chosen, I know that even if you stumble, you will not fail."

And he tells us this, "I will give you two gifts, to strengthen you in the midst of the conflict, and all along the way. First, you will have the presence of the Holy Spirit: the presence of the Father and the Son, dwelling within you to empower you, to give you courage and wisdom. Live in obedience to the Spirit's voice, and the Spirit's holiness will shine in you for all to see.

"And second, I give you the power of forgiveness. If you forgive the sins of anyone, they are forgiven, if you retain the sins of anyone, they are retained. Because they know the guilt of their own sins, people will believe Death when he lies to them and tells them that he will have the final word, that in the end he will have them. When they believe what he says, it will wrap chains around their hearts, chains just like the ones you have felt. But I have given you the power of forgiveness, and when you tell them how their sins can be forgiven, they will be set free."

As every preacher comes to know, more people will show up in church on Easter Sunday than any other day of the year. As we saw in the last chapter, the large crowd on Easter morning is not to be despised, but beloved. Do not give yourself permission, preacher, to be angry at these souls whom Jesus loves, who have managed to show up just once or twice over the course of the year.

Some of these people who show up on Easter morning are seekers who wonder whether the church has a message of hope to share in the face of death. Others will be seekers who wonder whether the church has any useful insight on the meaning or purpose for their lives. There is no better day for these seekers to come to church, for the Easter message is exactly what they need to hear. For the individual seeking solace and assurance, as we saw in chapter 8, Easter provides the confidence to move from fear and despair to hope and the promise of eternal life. For those seeking to understand the purpose of their existence, it is well to remember that Easter is also the story of how the risen Jesus sends forth his disciples with a message destined to change the world.

This sending forth does not happen all in a moment, of course. The sending of the church is prefigured in the sending of the disciples two by two, earlier during Christ's ministry. It is confirmed as Jesus addressed his followers just before he ascended, and demonstrated from Pentecost onward. But the specific turning point is Easter. Many of the Easter texts are, quite explicitly, missionary texts.

Throughout this book I have endeavored to show that as a preacher, you yourself hear the word of God speaking to you as you consider a story, often much more so than when you ponder on the original meaning of words in the biblical languages. A gain in understanding is always worthwhile — but the place where you hear God's voice will quite often be in the midst of the narrative.

That's probably even more true for the faithful members of your congregation than it is for you. Consider, then, how much more likely it is that those sporadic attenders will hear God addressing them in the midst of the flow of the narrative.

Their lack of participation in the church does not mean that they do not ponder on spiritual matters. Perhaps they ask the question in global terms, "What is the meaning of life?" Perhaps they ask it in individual terms, "What is the meaning of my life?" Or perhaps in colloquial terms, "What do I want to be when I grow up?" — a question asked by thirty- and fifty- and seventy-year-olds just as much as it is by ten-year-olds. You might feel like complaining that they ought to come to church more often if they want to find the answer, but you will be better served to recognize that some of them will be present this coming Easter, and they will be bringing that question in their souls when they show up.

In the 1640s, the Westminster Assembly wrote a *Confession of Faith*, a catechism for the instruction of adults, and a catechism for the instruction of children. The *Shorter Catechism* is perhaps a dozen pages in length. It provides 107 questions and answers that children were expected to memorize and recite, in order to have a solid grasp on the basic tenets of the Christian faith. The first of these reads:

> *Q1. What is the chief end of man?*
> *A. Man's chief end is to glorify God and enjoy him forever.*

This is a particularly fine statement regarding the purpose of human existence, capturing two critical ideas, joy and duty, in just a few words. Some philosophies propose pleasure as the highest good toward which we should direct our efforts, while other philosophies point us toward responsibility to the community or the nation. It's clear that the *Shorter Catechism*'s answer is similar to these, yet it is different in two important ways. First, it does not propose one unique notion as the highest good, to the exclusion of any other; it is both joy and duty at the same time. And second, the terms are not offered as abstract concepts; rather, they describe facets of a relationship. To glorify God — to point clearly and unambiguously to the reality that we are not here for ourselves, but to fulfill the gracious purpose of God almighty. To enjoy God forever — to be glad all the days of our lives and indeed throughout eternity in the fullness of being beloved and blessed of God.

Now this is not bad at all, as a brief and direct theological statement to instruct our minds. Still, that's different from being an encounter with God, to move our hearts. Moreover, its brevity works best when accompanied by some explanation. The catechism takes just eleven words to offer its answer to the question of the purpose of human existence. It took me 170 words to explain that answer, with its two parts of that answer, joy and duty, not as philosophical abstractions but as interwoven facets of our relationship to God.

There will be people who will come to church this Easter Sunday wondering, "What is the purpose of my life?" The risen Christ has an answer for them. His answer is this, "My purpose for your life is to send you forth as a joy-filled missionary in my name, to change the world."

But there is a credibility problem, preacher, if you simply state it like this. If you say, "Christ's purpose for your life is to send you forth as a joy-filled missionary in his name, to change the world," it is likely to sound like you are the one doing the sending, rather than Jesus.

On Easter, especially, you want to preach in narrative fashion where your hearers can identify their way into the story and sense God speaking to them, somewhere in the secret places of their souls. If they do genuinely hear the voice of the Lord addressing them, there is no guarantee that they will get everything right from now on (Peter and Judas both demonstrated that for us). Yet it remains our hope as preachers that they will leave the sanctuary with the prompting of the Spirit of God working in their souls, and not just the words of the preacher.

The preacher's goal cannot be to specify how each member of the congregation will fulfill their calling as a missionary. But we can earnestly hope that every member will leave with an ongoing conversation with God running in their soul, "All right, Lord, I believe you are calling me to fulfill part of your purpose to change the world. But, what am I to do, in response to this call?"

This might be done simply by telling part of the Jesus story, perhaps aiming toward a narrative exposition of John 20:21-23:

> *As the Father has sent me, so I am sending you. When he said this, he breathed on them and said to them, "Receive the Holy Spirit. If you forgive the sins of any, they are forgiven; if you retain the sins of any, they are retained."*

The idea in this text is plain enough. As the Father sent Jesus on this mission, so now he sends his followers on a mission, giving them two gifts to help them on their way: the presence of the Spirit, and the power of forgiveness. I present these verses, putting them in the form of a quest saga, to open this chapter.

Yet this critical theological understanding — Jesus the risen Lord now sends us out with his message — could equally well find narrative form in a series of contemporary parables.

Once upon a time, there was a dinner. It was a big dinner, and it was fancy. Table after table with beautiful white linens, crystal goblets, fine china. All the guests had arrived and found their seats. They had come from all over the world. Indeed, people had come from all down the centuries, for this was the great Feast of the Kingdom of God. From every people and tongue and tribe and nation, from all eras, all nations, all centuries — all the hungry hearts were gathered, gathered for the great Feast of the Kingdom.

But there was no food.

Well, there *was* food, but it was all still in the kitchen. There were great trays of beef tenderloin, cooked to perfection. Platters piled high with a hundred different kinds of vegetables, with all the best herbs and sauces. Baskets of bread. Rolls and muffins. Mini-loafs of corn bread. Golden popovers. And desserts. Cartloads of desserts.

All of the waiters were gathered in the kitchen, as well. The chief waiter, who was named Melissa, stood up on an overturned milk crate in the middle of the group. She looked around at all her crew and said, "When I tell you these things, I know I am simply reminding you of what you already know. Let's admit it, being a waiter is a demanding job. Sometimes you must move very fast. Sometimes you have to carry heavy loads. Sometimes you feel tired, and sometimes you feel unappreciated. Sometimes the tips aren't much.

"And yet, this is the most excellent job in the world! This is the job that delivers the food that the hungry people are longing for. What we do here is not about us. Indeed, we sometimes serve best when we are almost not noticed. After all," said Melissa, with laughter in her voice, "the people have come to the table for the Feast of the Kingdom, and not for the sake of the waiters! But the feast will not happen unless we, the waiters, deliver the food to these hungry souls, called to the feast.

"My friends," Melissa said to them, "this is a day to have great fun, fulfilling this task. This is the feast. The food is prepared. The hungry souls are ready. Now go. Go and serve the feast. Go and make the feast happen — the Feast of the Kingdom! Go! Go, and have great fun, as you make it happen."

Once upon a time, there was a wedding. The most beautiful bride, radiant, lovely. A tall and handsome groom. There they stood, trembling with devotion, devotion to each other, and devotion to the Lord whose love had drawn them together. The soloist sang a song so sweet, a song of hope and love. The bride spoke up, and offered her promises, in a voice clear and full of confidence. The groom spoke up, and offered his promises, in a voice clear and full of confidence.

Then they kissed. Ah, what a kiss! They kissed with a kiss so tender, so alive, it brought a tear to every eye and sent a shiver of gladness and wonder into every heart.

And after the kiss, the preacher spoke up, and said, "When I say these things to you, I know I am simply reminding you of what you already know. You are now husband and wife. The two of you have become one, in the fullness of God's love. Now go. Go in the joy of Christ our Lord. Go forth as this beloved couple that God has created you, and called you, and destined you to be. Go! Go and have great fun, as you live out in your human lives the wonder and splendor of the eternal love of God."

Once upon a time, there was a homecoming parade. It took place in a small town named Saint Ambrose. The town was founded during the great westward sweep of the pioneers, by devout people who remembered that the relatively unknown Saint Ambrose had been the teacher of the relatively famous Saint Augustine. When those pioneers founded their town, they dreamed of their role in educating future leaders. The day would come when they would establish a college, and then down the generations they would train great leaders and saints who would make their mark in history.

Then the railroad was built, and passed them by. Another town was selected as the county seat. The college that the town founders had hoped for never got established. In recent years, the town's population had been fairly stable, but whenever even one family moved away, it seemed to put a dent in the whole community's population, and in their morale.

The students of the high school in Saint Ambrose were known as the Saint Ambrose Saints. In years past, Friday night high school football games had been a major feature of community life, but a dozen or so years ago they had discontinued the football program. There had been some extended and sometimes painful debate about it, but the bottom line was, there just weren't enough boys who wanted to come out for a team that would be overmatched by every other team in the league.

Much to everyone's surprise, not having a football program turned out to be a good thing. Concentrating on springtime sports, the Saint Ambrose Saints now fielded pretty decent teams in boys' baseball and girls' softball, and they had developed an excellent high school marching band.

The marching band always led the annual Saint Ambrose Homecoming Parade. This year, though, *they were* the parade. People told themselves it was better this way. In years past there had been two or three small floats as well, but those floats were kind of embarrassing, really, usually assembled at the last moment. These would be nothing more than a hay wagon pulled by a tractor, with a few members of the Rotary Club sitting on hay bales, holding a banner and tossing candy to the children.

This year, though, there were no floats. Some people felt a pang of loss over this. Had it come to the point where they couldn't even get the Rotarians to put together an absolutely minimal float? Others thought maybe it was better this way; without those vaguely embarrassing floats tagging along, the parade would focus on those 37 members of the high school marching band. That meant, of course, that from the drum major in front to the three trombones bringing up the rear, the entire length of the whole parade would be thirty yards. Even so, they were truly a quality production, one in which their families and their community could take honest pride.

The parade route began at the gate of the cemetery on North Main, and proceeded south past the fire station, through the downtown area, and on to the high school — five blocks in all. As they marched to the fire station, the Saint Ambrose Saints would play "The Battle Hymn of the Republic." Then they would march on to downtown, playing the theme music from *Rocky*. Then they would proceed to the high school, playing their signature song. You've probably already guessed the title of their signature song: "When the Saints Go Marching In." Actually, "When the Saints Go Marching In" was like the signature song for the whole community. The song served as an emblem for so many things. It was part of the way the town cherished its heritage, across the generations. The song provided a powerful sense of religious connection, for those whose religion was steadfast and passionate. It provided a powerful sense of religious connection, for those whose religion was more sporadic. The song somehow drew households together, and made them feel the power of family more clearly. It drew the whole town together, and made them feel the power of being a community that functions as a great extended family. All of that, and more, held in those fiery words:

> *Oh when the saints go marching in!*
> *Oh when the saints go marching in!*
> *O Lord! I* want *to be in that number.*

The Saint Ambrose High School marching band gathered there on that beautiful fall morning, in the grassy area alongside the low stone wall, just outside the cemetery gate. Half a block south they could see the people of the town on both sides of the street, in front of the fire station — their parents and grandparents, brothers and sisters, cousins. Former members of the community had arrived in town the previous evening, to share in this annual homecoming celebration. People from other towns around would drive in to visit the Saint Ambrose homecoming just because it was such a wonderful event. There were a lot of people there, waiting for the parade to start.

The band members were feeling a little nervous. They had practiced their music, and they knew that they could play that music, but they also knew that with some regularity a wrong note would come forth. They didn't like it when a wrong note came forth. They had practiced their marching, and they knew they could march well, but they also knew that with some regularity, someone would be thinking about the music and would miss one of the flourishes or stutter steps. They didn't like it when someone got out of step. They were feeling a little nervous.

It was almost time. The drum major, Tony, hopped up on top of the low stone wall, there by the cemetery gate. He looked around at his schoolmates, standing proud in their band uniforms. The chatter faded to silence, and Tony said, "When I tell you these things, I know I am simply reminding you of what you already know. We have practiced. We know our music. We know how to march. We are ready. Now — let's go. Let's go and march. I want every one of you to go and play your music, with all your heart.

What if someone misses a step? Just keep on doing your best. What if someone plays a wrong note? Just keep on doing your best. Go! Go and march! Go, doing your very best. Go, and have great fun, so that all the world wants to be in that number, as the Saints go marching in."

Once upon a time, Jesus gathered his followers. The last chapter of the gospel of Matthew tells us this part of the story of Easter. It tells us how some of the women had gone to the tomb on Sunday morning, and discovered that Jesus had been raised from the dead. First the angels explained it to them. Then Jesus himself met them, and instructed them to tell his disciples to come and meet with him at the mountain in Galilee.

The women, with their hearts trembling with a great and fearsome joy, ran and told the other disciples what they had seen. They told them as well that Jesus wanted them to meet him on the mountain of Galilee. So they went; and in the wonder of Easter, in the glory of the resurrection, eleven disciples showed up to meet Jesus. Eleven. When they saw Jesus, their hearts were filled with joy, just as the hearts of the women had been, and they worshiped him. Some doubted, the Bible admits to us, quite frankly. Having some serious doubt did not rule out their presence. It was Easter, and eleven tentative followers of Jesus were there, with their hopes, their doubts, their faith, their nervousness.

What did Jesus say to them? I have to think that they talked for some little while, surely twenty or thirty minutes, on such a momentous occasion. It would not be surprising if the conversation went on for several hours. Matthew has summarized all that Jesus said in three short verses, which take less than thirty seconds to read out loud.

What, then, did Jesus say, from which Matthew has provided this terse summary? Obviously, we cannot say for sure, but I would suppose Jesus would have laughed in delight at the look of wonder on their faces. He would have told them once again how much he loved them. Perhaps with a twinkle in his eye he would even have said, "When I tell you these things, I know I am simply reminding you of what you already know. As my disciples you understand that I have died and risen so that you can know that all your sins are forgiven, and so that you can know that death is not the end of the story. You know this. There is a world out there that is aching to know it as well. Now go. Go and make disciples. Go to all the nations, and make disciples. Go! Go and baptize, go and teach. Go and have great fun, making disciples whose hearts are as full of joy as your hearts are."

Tony, the drum major, jumped down from the wall, and pointed his baton at the snare drum player who began to rattle out a drum roll so brisk it seemed to set the fire of God in the bones of each of the marchers, as they ran to their places. The bass drum began to pulse out the beat: *boom, boom, boom, boom* — and the Saint Ambrose Saints began to march, with those words ringing in their souls: "Go! Go and march!" And the fire of God kindled in the hearts of everyone lining the parade route, for they, too, wanted to be in that number, as the Saints go marching in.

With all his best drum major energy, Tony strutted at the front of the parade, his right arm like a piston as he kept the beat. He did not need to look back. By the sound in his ear and the fire in his soul he could tell that his schoolmates were playing their hearts out, the best they had ever done — they were the Saint Ambrose Saints, and they believed! It came ringing out in the music and in the marching — without even looking Tony could tell all this. Block by block they marched, then, as they came to the corner of the school yard, Tony turned around, marching backward in perfect precision, watching in blazing delight as the Saints came marching in to the high school driveway.

Oh! His eyes flared wide in wonder and astonishment, for behind the three trombones, he saw the whole town marching along. Arm in arm they came, some just walking, some of them briskly in step. Some of them singing along, some of them laughing in delight, some of them with tears on their cheeks. Marching! Marching like the saints of God, marching like the saints, when the saints go marching in to the kingdom!

Exercise 9-1

Choose one of the following, and use it to create the narrative framework for a motivational missionary Easter sermon.

1. Mark 16:1-8 — This is Mark's famous "broken ending," where the text stops in mid-sentence (εφοβουντο γαρ), prompting copyists in the second or third centuries to add some additional material to fill in "the rest of the story" (these additions have become known as the "longer ending" and the "shorter ending" of Mark). Suppose that it is not by accident that the text comes to us with this abrupt ending; suppose that Mark has deliberately broken the story off this way, in the knowledge that we who read the text will already know that this is not how the story ends. (That is, if we have been given a copy of this gospel that the church proclaims, we already know that there is an active group of people who proclaim a message about Jesus.) That causes a dissonance between the way the text ends and the reader's awareness of an ongoing community of proclamation. This dissonance prompts the question: When the women said nothing to anyone because they were afraid, was that the end of the story forever? Or did it turn out in the end that in spite of being afraid, the women told what happened, and the message of the gospel went forth to change the world? Based on this dissonance, create a narrative about a young mother in late-first-century Rome who has been given a copy of this gospel by the old widow who lives next door. Tell part of the story from the mother's perspective, as she ponders on how she might respond to the stirrings she feels in her heart when she reads about Jesus. Tell part from the neighbor's perspective, as she sympathizes with the young mother who lives next door.
2. Luke 24:44-49 — The most vanilla of the resurrection stories. Jesus said five things: about the Bible, the death and resurrection of the Messiah, proclamation of repentance and forgiveness to all nations, the identification of the witnesses, and the promise of the Spirit. The fourth

item simply says, "You are witnesses of these things" (v. 48 has just three words in the Greek: υμεις μαρτυρες τουτων). Witnesses are people who have seen something, and tell what they have seen. As a narrative exposition of this fourth point that the followers of Jesus are witnesses, put together three or four vignettes of individuals who have seen the grace of God in action, and told what they have seen. You might do this 1) by yourself telling the stories of those individuals, 2) by recruiting them to share those stories during worship, or 3) by setting them up as a panel discussion in the front of the sanctuary, with you acting as the host and interviewer, helping them tell their stories and interact with each other.

3. Acts 9:1-19; 1 Corinthians 15:1-8 — The story of Saul on the road to Damascus is generally read as a conversion story, but it should also be recognized as a story about how encountering the risen Christ turned Saul into a missionary. The events in Saul's narrative did not take place on Easter Sunday, so they point us toward the recognition that Easter kept on being Easter, even many years later. Create a story about a store manager, nurse, attorney, or machinist — one who is asking, "What is it that God wants me to do with my life?" Tell us how your hero begins to sense an answer to this question, yet still struggles with how this answer gets put into practice (which is to say, even an encounter with the risen Christ doesn't clear away all the doubts or make everything easy from here on out). Interweave the two narratives into a sermon in such a way that your hero's story becomes a parable that illumines the story of Saul's encounter with the risen Christ, and Saul's story becomes a parable that illumines the story of your hero.

So, preacher, when I tell you these things, I know I am simply reminding you of what you already know. Even so, I remind you. The kingdom of God is like a great feast, with all the world sitting down at table to celebrate. The kingdom of God is like a wedding, full of joy and promise, emblem of the passionate love of Jesus which establishes a whole new relationship. The kingdom of God is like a homecoming parade that begins at a cemetery and moves to a school, with a small band of believers playing "When The Saints Go Marching In" and everyone who hears it says, "Yes! O Lord, *I* want to be in that number!" And as they hear it and say it and join in, they become part of the march — they are in that number.

The kingdom of God is like Jesus telling his friends to go make disciples of all the nations.

The kingdom of God is like you, preacher, as you tell the story of Easter to the friends who will gather this coming Sunday.

Now go! Go to it! Go and preach that sermon — go and make disciples of those who will gather in the hope that they will hear God's answer to the question of the purpose of their existence. Go, preacher, go and have great fun, using the gifts our Lord has set within you to speak the words that will make disciples, who will go and make disciples in Jesus' name.

---

1. Some of the material in this chapter was originally published as "I Am Sending You," in James W. Cox, ed., *Best Sermons 6* (New York: HarperCollins, 1993).

Chapter 10

Once Upon A Christmas

preaching the doctrine of incarnation as a story

Once upon a time, there was an old man. His name was Martin Donovan. He had been an old man for a long time. His wife, Flora, had died a few years ago, and he missed her greatly, but he had been an old man before that. He still remembered the moment he became an old man. It was just a month after his 46th birthday, the day the Marine captain came to the house to tell him and Flora that their son, Daniel, had been killed in Vietnam.

Danny was a college graduate, a young officer, filled with life and such great potential. Martin had himself served in World War II, had fought as an infantryman in Europe. He had been wounded twice. He had seen his friends killed. He understood the terrible cost of war. Even so, he was proud of his service to his country, but never so proud as when his boy, Danny, received his commission as a lieutenant.

And six months later, Danny was dead. Even now, after thirty years had passed, there were days when Martin felt he would never recover from the grief. He still felt the pang of bitter questions about why America ever got involved in any war in Vietnam. At the same time, after all these years there were also days when Martin never thought about Danny at all. That was okay, he told himself; as Flora had always said, the living have to go on living. But telling himself didn't always work. Often he would feel terribly guilty, as if he had been disloyal to his son's memory, by letting two days go by without grieving for him.

While Flora was alive, Martin seemed to be doing pretty well. But after she died, in November of '93, Martin found himself going again and again to the cemetery, standing there, looking at the graves of his wife and his son ten days in a row, after Flora's funeral. Then it became a pattern of several times a week. He still did it.

He never wept. At least, he never wept that anyone could see. Sometimes his friend, Roger Morrison, went with him. Other times Roger made it a point to walk his retriever on the path across the cemetery so that he would happen to bump into Martin there. Roger never saw his friend say anything, in all the time he stood before those two side-by-side graves — neither to pray, nor to talk to his dead wife and son, as people often do in cemeteries, nor even to talk to himself. When he walked the dog, Roger would slow down a hundred yards away, to give Martin plenty of time to ponder or meditate or whatever was on his mind, before Roger's arrival interrupted him. As far as Roger could tell, all Martin did was stand at the foot of the two graves, staring at one headstone and then the other, with a haunted look in his eyes.

Juliana was one of those unpredictable young girls who constantly astonish you. At age thirteen, she was in the bloom of early adolescence, with eager intelligence and a bubbly energetic smile and depth of soul. Ever since she fell in love with Jesus at church camp two years ago, Juliana had become a sponge, hungry for knowledge and faith, soaking up understanding of what it means to be a disciple. There was so much right about her that it was easy to be angry at her, when she was wrong. It was sometimes easy to be angry at her, even when she was right. But Juliana was so irrepressibly cheerful it was hard to be angry at her for very long.

The Sunday before Thanksgiving, she overheard some of the ladies at church talking about Martin Donovan. "It's really a pity," they said. "I think he just sits at home most of the time. Well, he and Roger Morrison go to lunch every Tuesday. Roger says the grief and sadness in him is just so deep, but he never talks about it at all. I wish we could get Martin back to church. Of course, he wasn't all that active before, but I suppose he hasn't been here at all, since Flora's funeral."

That afternoon, Juliana told her mother what she had heard the church ladies saying about Martin Donovan, and then asked, "Why is he so sad?"

Her mother didn't answer right away. During the pause Juliana watched the shadows of emotions move across her mother's face. Then her mother said, "He has had a hard life. He misses his wife, who died a few years ago. You didn't have her for a Sunday school teacher, but you'll remember your brothers did."

Juliana nodded, all her attention focused on her mother's face. Her mother said, "And he misses his son, Danny, who died many years ago, in the Vietnam war."

Juliana read the twitch in the corner of her mother's mouth, and thought she knew what it meant. She asked, "Did you know his son?"

Juliana watched her mother smile as she nodded, "Yes. Danny was two years ahead of me in high school."

It felt a little awkward and embarrassing, but Juliana could sense an echo of deep mystery trembling in her veins. And so, greatly daring, she asked, "Were you in love with him?"

And this time her mother laughed, and said, "Oh, all of us girls were at least half in love with Danny Donovan, at one time or another. He was a handsome young man, he always had fun ideas, and he made us laugh. When he went off to college, we were all heartbroken. For a little while, anyway."

Juliana considered. She had already gleaned more information than she ever expected to get. Perhaps she should quit while she was ahead. But she decided to risk one more question, since her mother seemed to be in the right mood to answer. So Juliana asked, "Would you have married him?"

Her mother became so still. She didn't get mad, but she didn't answer, either. Juliana held her breath. Finally her mother said, "I don't know. A person never does know about things like that. Danny never asked me. If he had, I might have said, 'Yes.' As it turns out, I married someone else, and your two brothers are the result. And, as you know, that marriage didn't work out. It doesn't always work out. Then I married your father, and here we are."

Juliana thought about this story a lot, on the Monday and Tuesday and Wednesday before Thanksgiving. On Wednesday afternoon, she stopped at the grocery store on her way home from school. She bought a frozen pecan pie, took it home, and baked it. When it had cooled, Juliana walked the three blocks to Martin Donovan's house, rang the doorbell, and waited.

The old man came to the door. He looked at Juliana, and said, "What do you want?" With all her cheerfulness Juliana said, "Hi, Mr. Donovan. My name is Juliana Vernon, and I wanted to bring you a pie!"

Martin looked at her. He said, "I don't want to buy any pies today," and he started to close the door.

She said, "Please wait, Mr. Donovan. I'm not selling pies. This is for you, as a present for Thanksgiving. It's only a pie from the store, but I did bake it myself, just for you."

"Why?" he asked.

Juliana took a deep breath, and her words tumbled out in a rush as she said, "Because Jesus loves me, and I know he loves you, too, and so I baked a pie to bring to you, just because of the love of Jesus."

Martin took the pie. His voice was a little gruff, but he managed to thank her. He closed the door. He took the pie to the kitchen, and set it on the table.

Several times that evening he looked at the pie. He thought about it. He liked pecan pie, but he couldn't quite bring himself to cut into it. The pie sat on the kitchen table all night. On Thanksgiving morning, Martin put the pie in with the kitchen trash and carried the bag out to the garbage can.

He didn't know why he did that. Part of his soul was astonished that some young teenager would bring him a pie, for the love of Jesus or for any other reason. Part of his soul felt so angry that anyone would have pity on him. And part of his soul felt ashamed, for spurning her innocent gift. In the shaving mirror he told his reflection, "You've become a bitter old man."

Each year, starting sometime in November, American culture begins its annual flirtation with Christmas. It is an awkward dance. As a nation we are both confused and fascinated by Christmas. Some people say it is a religious holiday, and therefore insist that governmental organizations — including elementary school music programs and city hall lawn displays — must offer neither support nor endorsement for it. Others insist that Christmas is mostly an American wintertime holiday about Santa Claus and elves, about snow and family and children's toys, and maybe world peace; and so, since it isn't actually all that religious, then there ought to be a way to have a manger in front of city hall, and to have the children sing "Away In The Manger" for their winter choral concert — just as part of the heritage of the event, without *really* saying anything terribly religious thereby.

Arguments along these lines about freedom of religion sometimes make the headlines, but perhaps the political debate is less important than the economic one, in terms of figuring out the meaning of Christmas. Altruistic retailers urge us to spend robustly at Christmas, in order to keep the national economy strong; while family members reckon with their own greediness and their desire to be a little more frugal this year than last, and their hope that if they can find and buy just the right present they will be able to bring joy to someone's heart. Meanwhile, each of us is secretly wondering whether this year that special someone might just possibly have found the way to give us The Gift that will truly bring joy to our own hearts.

Amidst all this personal and political and economic and cultural confusion, we encounter a wide variety of Christmas stories. It is an interesting feature of contemporary American life that by and large these are no longer stories we tell; they have mostly become movies that we watch. Only a few of these Christmas stories contain any moments at all that are recognizably Christian.

A number of films seem to want to tell yet another tale about Santa Claus. When this happens, the narrative has usually been shifted so thoroughly that it is difficult to discover any similarity to the original legend of Niklaus, fourth-century Bishop of Myra, who gave gifts to people in need, and did so with such anonymity that no one has ever been able to tell for sure whether it was indeed Niklaus or somebody else who brought the present that met that need. The original legends about Niklaus, rather than tales about the North Pole guy who brings you toys if you have been good all year long, these are what we should be telling to our children.

Exercise 10-1

Niklaus (280?-351), bishop of Myra, a small city on what is now the south coast of Turkey, may have been in attendance at the Council of Nicaea (325). Very little actual information is known about his life, but the legends about Saint Niklaus become the background for the generous giver who became known in different countries as Saint Nicholas and Santa Klaus / Santa Claus.

The most famous incident is one in which it came to Niklaus' attention that an impoverished family with three daughters was going to be forced to sell the girls into slavery. (To a brothel owner, actually. You can skip over that part if you don't wish to explain it to the youngest children, but it is part of the story that teens and adults should probably get to find out about.) On successive nights, it is said, Niklaus tossed a small sack of coins through the open window of this family's hut; this provided the dowry to allow each of the girls to marry, thus enabling them to live normal lives. The "it is said" part is important — no one saw him do it — thus even though people figured out that it was (probably) Niklaus, no one has ever known for sure exactly where these gifts came from.

Select one of the following, and do it as an oral exercise:

1. Tell the story of Niklaus of Myra as a children's sermon, focusing on this idea — we never really know for sure if a present comes from Santa Claus, because when Saint Niklaus gave gifts no one saw him do it; but whenever we give gifts and no one knows for sure where they came from, we follow the pattern that Saint Niklaus set for us.
2. Tell the story of a mother telling her children the story of Niklaus of Myra, as she explains to them that "other families remember the story of Saint Niklaus in different ways, but in our family we remember his generosity this way." Include these ideas: Santa Claus does not bring gifts to us, because we are not poor — we give gifts to each other, because we can express our love for each other this way. We follow the example of Santa Claus by giving anonymous gifts to help change the lives of people who have no other source of help.

Not all the stories that come to us during the weeks leading up to Christmas focus directly on Santa Claus. Others present us with characters with some peripheral relationship to Santa Claus — elves and reindeer, for example — or on characters created for the sake of telling Christmas stories that don't have anything to do with Jesus — snowmen, scrooges, and grinches. (The slogan for these storytellers appears to be "Keep Christ out of Christmas.")

What does it mean that there should be such a variety of stories being told? A cynic might propose that it is all about money. The moviemakers believe they can turn a profit by cranking out yet another feel-good sentimental Christmas movie, and what do you know? It pays off for them, yet again.

Yet if it is indeed about money, let me suggest that it is not quite *all* about money. The reason moviemakers can turn a profit creating new Christmas tales is this: American culture has never lost its deep yearning to hear at Christmas a story, a story that will move people's hearts. What they get is usually only a shadow of what they long for, but the moviemaking marketers have indeed correctly discerned that there is a story that needs to be told at Christmas.

It falls to you, preacher, to find a way to tell stories at Christmas that touch that yearning, and thereby put people in touch with the Christmas story, with all its depth, complexity, and resolution.

Exercise 10-2

Consider the following scripture readings: Luke 1:5-25, 57-80; Galatians 4:4-5; Isaiah 9:2-7; Matthew 1:18-2:23; Luke 1:26-56, 2:1-20. Be sure (as always) to take the time to read the text *out loud*. Read it with a different voice each time. For example, read it as a nervous middle-schooler making an oral report in class, or as a bored department manager giving an orientation lecture to trainees that would rather not be there, or as an oily politician pretending to be sincere, or as a young soldier sharing an important family story with his comrades before a battle in which they will all probably die, or as a frail great-grandmother recounting ancient wisdom to her great-grandchildren. As always, notice how your tone of voice affects the meaning of the words.

Then choose one of the following:

1. Read Luke 1:5-25, 57-80 two or three more times. Now tell the story of Zechariah, in your own words. You need to include some details about Elizabeth, but focus on Zechariah's feelings. How does he like his role in temple worship? What is his prayer life like? What does he feel when he encounters the angel? Tell us Zechariah's story, in a way that will let us see his faith and his frustration, and also see why he answered the way he did, both to Gabriel and also to those who objected that the baby should not be named John.
2. Read Luke 1:5-25, 57-80 two or three more times. Now tell the story of Elizabeth, in your own words. You need to include some details about Zechariah, but focus on Elizabeth's feelings. How does she feel about being childless? What are her emotions when Zechariah comes home from temple duty unable to speak? Tell us Elizabeth's story in a way that will let us see her faith and her frustration, and also see how her heart responds when she begins to suspect that she might just possibly be pregnant, and also how she felt when the relatives were objecting to the name she gave the baby.
3. Read Galatians 4:4-5 two or three more times. Notice the following ideas: the fullness of time, God sending his Son, the birth of the Son and God's purpose of redeeming those who stand condemned under the law. Now tell the story of the incarnation from the perspective of the triune God. Include God's perspective on several of the following: Abraham, Moses, the judges, David, Hosea, Jeremiah, Ezekiel. Focus on God's longing to redeem these lost sinners, leading to God sending the Son, born of woman, to redeem.
4. Read Isaiah 9:2-7 two or three more times. Notice the following ideas: light for those whose way is shrouded in darkness, joy and freedom at the joyous conclusion of a bloody battle, the birth of a Son who personifies four names

(Mighty God is one of those names; Everlasting Father, Prince of Peace, and Wonderful Counselor are the other three names), the purpose for which this Son is born of establishing peace and righteousness forever, the passion of the Lord, *qannah*, to make this come true. Now tell the story of the incarnation of the Son who is born to us, and of what the passionate love of the mighty God would accomplish thereby for those whose life is again and again in conflict and darkness — tell it from the perspective of Isaiah, who has been granted just a glimpse of this story by the Everlasting Father, Prince of Peace, Wonderful Counselor.

5. Read Matthew 1:18—2:23 two or three more times. Now tell the story of Joseph, in your own words. You need to include some details about Mary, but focus on Joseph's role. Notice that a great deal of "the Christmas story as we know it" does not get told here. There are no shepherds, there is no choir of angels, no trip to Bethlehem, no inn, no manger. The main character is Joseph — a righteous man who dreams dreams, discerns that these dreams are messages from God, and takes action in response. Consider how Joseph's understanding of his own identity may have been shaped as he grew up by listening to the story of the patriarch Joseph, also an interpreter of dreams. Notice that you can tell the Christmas story focused in on just one character; that's what Matthew has done.

6. Read Luke 1:26-56, 2:1-20 two or three more times. Now tell the story of Mary, in your own words. You need to include some details about Joseph, but focus on Mary's role. Notice that a great deal of "the Christmas story as we know it" does not get told here. There are no wise men, there is no hubbub in Jerusalem nor a jealous King Herod, there is no anxiety on the part of Joseph about his already-pregnant fiancée. The main character is Mary, a devout teenage servant of the Lord who sings hymns that magnify the Lord, ponders events in the quietness of her heart, and accepts a calling to bear what most of us would consider to be an intolerable burden. Tell the story of Mary. Notice,

again, that you can tell the Christmas story focused in on just one character; that's what Luke has done.

On Wednesday afternoon, the week after Thanksgiving, Martin Donovan heard his doorbell ring again. When he opened it, there stood that same girl, saying, "Hi, Mr. Donovan! It's me, Juliana Vernon again. This time I brought you an apple pie." There was so much enthusiasm in her smile as she held it out to him that he just had to take it. She said, "I hope you like it, but I've got a big test to study for, so I have to run." And she scurried down the sidewalk and around the corner.

Martin stood there in the doorway, astonished. His arm trembled. He closed the door, leaned against the inside of the door, and looked at the top of the pie. Juliana had carved a picture in the top crust, for the steam vents — a few stark lines to form a stable, a curved line suggesting a hillside in the background, and a bright star shining in the night sky overhead.

In a sudden rage, he hurled the pie down the hall, where it crashed against the kitchen doorpost. He was immediately ashamed. He stared at the mess. Why had he done that? He got a bucket and brush and mop, and cleaned up the ruined pie from the wall and floor. And listened to his conscience mocking him: "Bitter old man. Bitter old man. Bitter old man."

In order for Good Friday and Easter to have their full impact on our lives, the doctrine of the cross and resurrection needs to become interwoven into our understanding of who we are. An understanding of the doctrine of the incarnation functions the same way with regard to Christmas. The gospel of John therefore begins by offering a theological explanation for why Jesus came to this world. The great prologue tells of the Word of God, present with God, indeed being God, taking on genuine human flesh; he is the true light who comes to give light to all the world (John 1:1-18). He comes to give light and life and grace and truth to each one of us. That's what the opening verses of John's gospel tell us.

It also tells us, despite the astonishing quality of these gifts, it is not automatic that they will be received.

This insight will not come as completely new information for most of us. As it turns out, many people in this world have intuitively gleaned an awareness of these two points that the gospel teaches: 1) there are great gifts, and yet 2) the gifts might not get received.

There's more to it than just this intuitive awareness, though. In order to be complete, the insight needs to make a theological connection — the theological connection that recognizes that it is not simply that there are great gifts, but that these gifts come from a giver; namely, these gifts are presented by God Almighty, offered in deep compassion and in earnest longing for the redemption of all people. It also needs to make an existential connection — the existential connection that recognizes it is not simply that some random gifts out there might not get received, but these gifts which have been offered *to me — by God —* might not get received because *I might fail* to recognize or accept them.

This intuitive awareness — that there are great gifts, and that they might not get received — quite often has not yet been explored theologically or existentially. Indeed, it may not yet have been fully articulated. I am sure, preacher, that you have experienced this on many occasions — sometimes intuitive appreciations remain in a holding pattern at the pre-articulate level for quite some time. That is, you really do have these insights, even though you have never put into words. When the day comes that you do express it for yourself for the very first time, you feel the sense of newness as you put this into your own words, and you also feel the reality that you are saying something that you have known within your soul for a long time.

It falls to preachers, each year when the month of December rolls around, to proclaim the gospel of the birth of the Savior to the various people who show up in the sanctuary. It is a mixed crowd, isn't it? Among them there will be some individuals who do not attend worship too often. They are officially members of the church, but generally they show up only on Easter Sunday and perhaps on one or two of the Sundays leading up to Christmas day. Some others will be present, because of ongoing family affiliation; for many years they have not lived in town — and for many years they have not lived as part of a community of faith — but sometimes they come back to visit their grandmothers; and when they do, the whole family comes to church on Christmas Sunday or Christmas Eve. At the same time there are those who worship faithfully several dozen Sundays a year. They are dedicated members, they are hard workers, and they find themselves needing to hear again that the coming of Jesus is good news, and not simply more work they have to do so that other people can have a good time at Christmas.

As I have suggested earlier, it is no easy task to offer a teaching sermon to the typical American congregation on an ordinary Sunday because

- as a society we have taught ourselves to have a very limited attention span for information presented in lecture form; and because
- most Christians have such low expectations for themselves regarding their own ongoing learning of scripture's content and doctrine, and so year by year they do not know their Bibles any better; and because
- the preacher therefore does not have very many "Bible building blocks" that can be used to form a quick sketch of the shared biblical heritage of the congregation; and because
- even within a congregation where the range of Bible students could be classed as absolute beginners, beginners, and advanced beginners — no midrange or advanced students to worry about — that still spans a wide enough spectrum of knowledge and understanding that most any moment in the teaching will be boring to some people and over the heads of others.

If this is true on an average Sunday morning, the problem is not less with the significantly more-diverse congregation on the Sunday before Christmas, or on Christmas Eve itself. Yet this is the moment to teach the doctrine of the incarnation. These people who long to hear the story of Christmas deserve to experience this: The Word of God, who took on our human existence and came to live among us long ago, still comes to encounter us in our human existence today, and will live among us and within us. A great gift, which might not get received.

Yet if they have somehow not quite connected with this gift previously, it still remains possible for them to receive it now.

Martin Donovan sat in his living room, the Wednesday after he had thrown the pie down the hall. He wondered if his doorbell would ring once again with that girl who had brought him those two pies — "for the love of Jesus." But the doorbell did not ring. Nor did it ring the next day. Martin told himself that he was glad the girl had given up. He did his best not to notice that he also felt — a little disappointed.

And then Juliana showed up late Friday afternoon, with a pumpkin pie.

"Why do you keep bringing me these damn pies?" he said, harshly, hating himself for his harshness.

His voice was intimidating, but Juliana refused to let herself be scared away. "There are two reasons, Mr. Donovan. The first I told you before: Because the love of Jesus just makes me want to do stuff like this. And the second is, because if things had been different, you might have been my grandfather."

Martin stood riveted in silence, his eyes glaring. Juliana pretended not to notice, as she said, "Of course I know how it works. If your son had married my mother, none of the children they might have had would ever have been me. I would never have been born. Or my brothers either. And yet it could have happened that way. So I'm kind of like the granddaughter you could have had."

It took Martin three tries before he could make words come out. Even so, his voice sounded like a croak as he asked, "Who is your mother?"

"Cassie Vernon."

Martin closed his eyes for a long moment. Then he asked, "Back in high school her name was Cassie MacNamara, wasn't it?"

Juliana nodded. They stood there, looking at each other in silence. Then she said, "Umm, Mr. Donovan, there is a third reason; I want to invite you to come sit with me and my family at church on Christmas Eve. Please."

He said, "Oh, child, you don't understand. You can't invite me to church." And then, hating himself, Martin went on, "You don't even know I threw away the two pies you brought me before."

Juliana lifted up her pumpkin pie, and said, "Maybe you'll like this one better." And she handed it over with such earnestness that he just had to take it — then she turned and fled for home.

The doctrine of the incarnation teaches us of this astonishing way that grace is offered to us, along with the recognition that we need to find the way to receive this grace. People need to understand this doctrine; yet you will not need to provide all that much doctrinal information in order for them to get it. (Naturally enough, there will be some individuals who want to explore the meaning of the incarnation in much more depth, but that's what Sunday school classes and topical studies are for.)

In this chapter I have provided just a few short paragraphs of theological and existential reflection (the recognition that the gifts of grace come from God, and need to be recognized and received by each individual). Yet didn't you already get just about everything you needed about that, just from the story of Juliana and Martin Donovan? For most of us gathered on Christmas Eve, we may just need to hear a few words to help us know that the light of the world can bring light to our lives once more; someone who can tell us, as Juliana put it, "Jesus loves me, and I know he loves you too, and so I baked a pie to bring to you, just because of the love of Jesus."

Late in the afternoon, the last day of school before Christmas, Juliana showed up at Martin's door with a peach pie. She handed it to him. They looked at each other. Neither spoke. Then she asked, "Will you come to Christmas Eve service, Mr. Donovan, and sit with me and my family?"

He summoned up all his courage, and said, "Juliana, I don't know."

The fourth pew seemed to have become the Vernon family pew; it was where Juliana's family always sat. On Christmas Eve, her older brother and his wife and their new baby, Lisa, sat on the aisle, so they could escape to the nursery if the baby started to cry. Next to them sat her brother, Richard, home from college. Then

Juliana's father, holding hands with her mother, the two of them glancing at each other from time to time as if sharing some wonderful secret only they knew. Juliana sat beside her mother. On the outside end of the pew sat Roger Morrison and his wife. And in between Roger and Juliana, Martin Donovan was there. He did not sing any of the hymns. He did not seem to be able to say anything at all. He was simply there, part of the family, sharing in the grace of Christmas Eve.

Exercise 10-3

Create your own Christmas story, a parable of the incarnation.

First, select a text from Exercise 10-2, or another of your choosing. What is the moment in this portion of the story of the incarnation that particularly speaks to you? Why is that?

Second, decide on a central character — perhaps one of the following or one of your own creation.

1. Eddie, a 51-year-old house painter, who had been married for 23 years when his wife divorced him. He always thought he was okay as a husband and father. He knew he was not the most romantic or the most perceptive fellow ever to come along, but he thought of himself as a regular guy who worked hard to be a good provider. One day his wife said "something was missing." She said "the magic was gone," whatever that meant. He still works hard; he'll paint your house outside or in, and month-by-month he sends alimony checks to his ex-wife. In the meantime, she seems to have convinced his son and daughter that the divorce was his choice and his fault. He figures there's always enough blame to go around, and there's no point in making bad matters worse by trying to convince the kids it was really all her fault.
2. Tom or Marilyn, a couple in their sixties. (Choose Tom or Marilyn — not both.) They are hosting the Christmas day festivities for their three children and their families. They have covered the living room and the den with stacks and

stacks of Christmas presents. But, is it enough? Have they bought enough that everyone will be happy? They each have memories of being very happy on Christmas morning. They each have memories of being disappointed. On balance, they have more memories of being disappointed. They have been disappointed by each other quite a few times and they carry a certain weight of guilt for that, although they would be reluctant to admit to that. Perhaps part of the question in their minds is, "If we have enough presents, if we make everyone happy this year, will that make up for some of those years when I didn't do a good enough job at making him or her happy?"

3. Cheryl, a 37-year-old single mother of two teenage boys. (Fill in these necessary details: Is Cheryl divorced, widowed, never-married? Where does she work? Does she like her job? What are the boys' names and ages?) As Christmas draws near, Cheryl feels pressured by her own weariness, and by her desire to make Christmas "happy" for her sons, and by her recognition that she doesn't really have the money to spend a lot on Christmas, and by the awareness that she needs to buy them clothes and school supplies instead of game equipment.

Third, consider what your character will do, and why. Will Tom decide to drive to the mall, to do just a little more last-minute shopping? Will Cheryl try to find an additional part-time job, so that she has a little more money to spend on her boys? What conflicts will your character encounter — conflicts with other people, with exterior circumstances, or within their own souls?

Fourth, discover just how it is, in the course of your character's story, that they encounter the kind of grace suggested in your Bible passage.

Fifth, tell that story.

www.ingramcontent.com/pod-product-compliance
Lightning Source LLC
Chambersburg PA
CBHW061256110426
42742CB00012BA/1944